FAMILY LITER.

Family Literacies demonstrates, through reference to empirical research, how shared reading practices operate in a wide range of families, with a view to supporting families in reading with their pre-school children. At the heart of this book, written by two highly experienced experts in the field, is a fascinating project that captured diverse voices and experiences by parents, children and other family members.

Rachael Levy and Mel Hall deploy a rich and distinctive theoretical framework, drawing on insights from literacy studies, education and sociology. *Family Literacies* presents an account of shared reading practices in homes, focusing attention on what motivates parents to read with their children as well as revealing what parents may need if they are to begin and sustain shared reading activity. The authors show the many ways in which reading is centrally embedded in many aspects of family life, arguing that this has particular implications for children as they start school. Situated within a socio-cultural discourse, this book explains why it is important to understand how and why shared reading takes place in homes so that all families can be supported in reading with their children.

Family Literacies is essential reading for all those who are studying and researching literacy practices, especially those involving young children. The book will also be of value to students, practitioners and researchers in education and applied linguistics who are working with families and have an interest in the study of family practices. The authors' findings have major implications for how parents can be encouraged to develop positive reading relationships with their children.

Rachael Levy is Associate Professor at UCL Institute of Education. She has published widely in the field of young children's reading and is the author of *Young Children Reading at Home and at School*. She has worked closely with the United Kingdom Literacy Association and was editor for their Minibook series for eight years.

Mel Hall is a Senior Lecturer in Childhood and Education Studies at Manchester Metropolitan University. Mel's research has been devoted to lived experiences of young people and families, with a particular emphasis on how health and education are conceptualised in the context of the life course.

LITERACIES

Series editors: Julia Gillen, Lancaster University, UK and Uta Papen, Lancaster University, UK

This long-established series publishes innovative and high-quality research and scholarship in the field of literacy studies. *Literacies* provides a home for books on reading and writing, which consider literacy as a social practice and which situate it within broader institutional contexts. The books develop and draw together work in the field; they are accessible, interdisciplinary and international in scope, and cover a wide range of social and institutional contexts.

For more information about this series, please visit: www.routledge.com/Literacies/book-series/LITERACIES

FAMILY LITERACIES

Reading with Young Children

Rachael Levy and Mel Hall

Routledge
Taylor & Francis Group
LONDON AND NEW YORK

First published 2021
by Routledge
2 Park Square, Milton Park, Abingdon, Oxon OX14 4RN

and by Routledge
605 Third Avenue, New York, NY 10158

Routledge is an imprint of the Taylor & Francis Group, an informa business

© 2021 Rachael Levy and Mel Hall

British Library Cataloguing-in-Publication Data
A catalogue record for this book is available from the British Library

Library of Congress Cataloging-in-Publication Data
Names: Levy, Rachael, author. | Hall, Mel, author.
Title: Family literacies: reading with young children/Rachael Levy and Mel Hall.
Description: New York: Routledge, 2021. | Series: Literacies |
Includes bibliographical references and index.
Identifiers: LCCN 2020048362 |
Subjects: LCSH: Reading (Early childhood)–Parent participation.
Classification: LCC LB1139.5.R43 L48 2021 | DDC 372.4–dc23
LC record available at https://lccn.loc.gov/2020048362

ISBN: 978-1-138-48845-8 (hbk)
ISBN: 978-1-138-48847-2 (pbk)
ISBN: 978-1-003-16372-5 (ebk)

Typeset in Sabon
by Newgen Publishng UK

TO MY MUM, KATE HART, WHO READ TO ME.
THANK YOU (RACHAEL)

TO MY NEPHEW NATHAN FOR ALL YOU HAVE TAUGHT ME.
LOVE, AUNTIE MEL (MEL)

CONTENTS

ILLUSTRATIONS

Figures

Table

ACKNOWLEDGEMENTS

We are very grateful to Julia Gillen, Director of the Literacy Research Centre and series editor, for her very thoughtful comments on the first draft of this book and her unwavering enthusiasm and encouragement throughout the process. She has undeniably had a major influence on the structure and quality of this book.

We are also very grateful to the Economic and Social Research Council (ESRC) for funding the study upon which this book is based. As described in Chapter 4 this study was part of a broader programme of research titled 'Promoting Language Development by Shared Reading', funded by the ESRC, grant number ES/M003752/1, and led by the University of Liverpool from 2015 to 2018. We are particularly grateful to Caroline Rowland for her skilled leadership of the overall project. We would also like to thank Josie Billington and Jamie Lingwood who we worked closely with during the three years of the study and whose work has influenced aspects of this study.

We extend gratitude to The Reader Organisation who played a valuable role in connecting us with participants and whose work remains an inspiration.

A special and heartfelt thanks goes to Jenny Preece who conducted many of the interviews which were so critical to the study and this book. Without Jenny's skill in encouraging so many parents to talk freely about their shared reading practices in the home, the study would not have yielded such rich data.

Of course, this book would not exist if it wasn't for the involvement of the many families who so generously gave their time to talk to us about their lives, their children and their shared reading practices. We really do thank you all so much.

Thank you 'Suzy' for allowing us to share your valuable story which features in the Conclusion of this book.

We would also like to thank Shivonne Gates for her time in reading Chapter 3 and for her very helpful comments on this.

Finally it is fair to say that the publishing team at Routledge have been a pleasure to work with and we are especially grateful to Eleni Steck for her regular communication and her gentle and supportive manner throughout the process.

Rachael's acknowledgements:

I would like to extend special thanks Jackie Marsh who has played a significant role in my career. Having examined my PhD in 2008, Jackie then kindly agreed to be my mentor for an ESRC-funded Post-Doctoral Fellowship at the University of Sheffield. This fellowship year then progressed into a further eight years at Sheffield where I worked as a Lecturer in Early Childhood Education. It was during this time that Jackie urged me to begin work on this book, so I will always be grateful for this encouragement. I wish to thank my many colleagues at Sheffield whose support and friendship sustained me and made me continue to endure the four-hour commute between Cambridge and Sheffield for as long as I did. It is at this point that I must give a special mention to my colleague who swiftly became my great friend, Jools Page. Thank you, Jools, for the amazing collaboration, friendship and fun we had at Sheffield and continue to have today.

I am very grateful to colleagues who I have met more recently at UCL Institute of Education, where I now work as an Associate Professor. I am particularly grateful to colleagues within the International Literacy Centre for their passion for literacy research – this has had a major impact on my writing of this book.

I am also very grateful for my contact with the United Kingdom Literacy Association (UKLA) over the years. I have benefitted hugely from the connections I have made through UKLA; this has included my participation at UKLA conferences and the privilege of working as an editor for the UKLA Minibook series for eight years.

Thank you to Mel, my co-author, for your dedication to this study and your contribution to this book. Your work with families has brought important sociological knowledge to this research, which has brought new perspectives to the study of reading in homes. I will always be grateful for this.

I also wish to thank my family for their continued interest and support as I have written this book. Thank you to my husband Nicholas Levy who has remained by my side throughout the journey and has very much supported from the sidelines. Many thanks to my (grown up!) children Daniel and Ben who have offered amazing encouragement throughout and quickly learned how to say 'the right thing' when writing was slow! I would also like to thank my sisters Debbie and Jennie who have been very encouraging of the writing – even though they did eat my own children's books when they were babies! It is impossible to mention all of the friends who have shown constant interest and enthusiasm for the writing of this book, from its inception to publication. But I would just like to mention Lynda, Heidi, Athena and Mony (otherwise known as 'The Art Group') who have all given me tremendous support – and have also lubricated the process with prosecco! Thank you.

Mel's acknowledgements:

I would like to express my profound gratitude to Pat Sikes for initially bringing me into the University of Sheffield School of Education fold in 2014. Being a Research Associate with Pat was my gateway to exploring family sociology with young people who have a parent with dementia. This became pivotal to my contribution in this book as well as being the reason I shared a corridor with Rachael and learned about this project in the first place. Pat, you gave me more love and confidence than I realised I needed or was even possible.

Thank you to my co-author Rachael for bringing me onto the project. Not only did it keep me in employment in precarious times, but it opened up a new area to me and resulted in my moving to Manchester. More than anything, working alongside you has been inspiring and allowed me to grow. I am looking forward to where we go next. Thank you for helping me realise 10-year-old Mel's dream and for being such a good friend.

I would like to thank colleagues at Manchester Metropolitan University for their support. In particular, my thanks go to Kate Pahl for her constant encouragement and enthusiasm for this research.

I must also mention Lauren White for her unwavering text support and for plugging the gaps in my sociological knowledge. Careers in academia are impossible without a best friend who 'gets it' and Lauren is mine. One day, I'll return the favour.

Finally, to my family. Dad, you might have never read a book, but you have never forgotten to ask 'How is the book going?'. It went well Dad! Thank you for all you have done to make this possible. To my sister, Louise, thank you for all your encouragement. Love you both.

1

READING WITH YOUNG CHILDREN: AN INTRODUCTION

When we think of children's reading, as an image, we are faced with a magnitude of possibilities. We may think of small chubby hands clutching a board book, or a teenager engrossed in a tale of wizardry. We might picture shelves of brightly coloured picture books in a library or bookstore, or we might see a child reading from a digital device. Some might see a five-year-old struggling to sound out a word in a reading scheme book, or a thirteen-year-old anxiously waiting to see if they will be asked to read aloud during an English lesson. Or we might see a parent reading a bedtime story to a child. Whatever images come to mind we can be assured that 'children's reading' is not a fixed concept. It can be a hobby, a task, a treat, a skill or a challenge. It can be the reward at the end of a busy day or it can be a chore to be confronted, endured or even avoided. It would be reasonable to suggest that those who are interested enough in children's reading to pick up this book, probably share a common desire for children to become confident, enthusiastic and independent readers, but it would be a mistake for us, the writers of this book, to assume that we share a universal understanding of what reading actually is and what is needed to help children to engage with reading. The very fact that reading carries a multitude of definitions is a recurring theme in this book and will be addressed in detail.

One important, but surprisingly under-researched activity, which features in the reading lives of some children, is that of reading with young children. Drawing extensively on a research study which was designed to investigate family reading practices, this book examines motivations and barriers to shared reading activity in homes. As authors, our interest in this topic stems from a variety of sources, both professional and personal. It would not surprise anyone to learn that we both enjoy reading as a leisure activity and our informal conversations with one another will often include reference to what we are currently reading, or a recommendation for a particular novel. Mel often speaks of the reading lives of her undergraduate students and is developing this as a research interest. In addition, both Rachael and Mel share an interest in young children's reading, having worked together on the study reported in this book. This study built on previous research that

Rachael has carried out, much of which has focused on the ways in which home and school discourses shape children's perceptions of reading; however, Rachael's specific interest in shared reading in the home has also evolved from her own personal history as evident in the following vignette.

Rachael's Story

I grew up in a small flat, in a quiet town in the south west of Scotland. My parents were not readers; our home had few books and those that we did have tended to be 'information books' rather than fictional texts. What is more, these books were rarely read, evident in the fact that they often got used to prop up unstable furniture, or, on one particularly unfortunate occasion, balance a fish tank, which resulted in the book becoming so wet that the pages morphed into one gloopy lump. Yet 'story' was a valued feature within my own childhood. Despite limited funds, children's books were purchased, and these stories were read. My mother read to me regularly; bedtime stories were prioritised; however, shared reading could happen at any time of the day. My father rarely read to me; however, he did tell stories of magical adventures of falling into strange lands (which I now recognise as being shamelessly based on Alice in Wonderland!).

I became a passionate reader throughout my primary years. Some of my fondest memories are of going shopping with my mother and returning with a new Enid Blyton book (or whole set of books on one particularly joyful occasion) accompanied by a packet of chocolate raisins. I read these books over and over again, never questioning the disparity between the lives of the characters in the books and my own world (tuck-boxes and lacrosse did not feature in my own education) but simply enjoying the stories.

What I didn't realise at the time was that this passion for reading was not only a hobby, but was also laying a foundation for my eventual career, which has included research into children's perceptions of reading. Of course it is not possible to say with any certainty that my professional life developed as a direct consequence of being read to as a young child; however, as a researcher of literacy practice, I cannot help but reflect on this relationship. I feel fairly certain that I benefitted hugely from being read to as a child, but as my interest in shared reading practices has developed, I have started to ask questions about parents' motivations for reading with their children. On a personal level, I do wonder what prompted my own mother to read regularly with me, despite the fact that she did not read for pleasure herself at the time (sadly she is no longer around, so I cannot ask this question to her directly). Given that this was a home where educational achievement was rarely discussed, I don't believe the activity was situated in a desire for educational endeavour.

This raises very interesting questions for me about the reasons why parents, and particularly those living in disadvantaged communities, do or do not read with their children. There really is a need for some research into this....

This book is about reading with young children. However, any discussion about reading practices must first begin with an exploration of the term 'reading'. In particular it is important to reflect on the ways in which definitions of reading have changed over the years and consider the implications of this for children's present and future reading. We therefore begin with an exploration of the term 'reading', before moving on to the concept of 'shared reading'. The social and emotional benefits of shared reading are acknowledged before we turn to look at existing research into shared reading practices.

What is reading?

In recent years reading has tended to be conceptualised in terms of 'skill' and 'will'; to put it simply, this means having the practical skills needed to decode print and make sense of text and the motivation (will) to want to read (Logan et al., 2011; Medford & McGeown, 2011). Focusing attention on the concepts of 'skill' and 'will' does help to establish how many researchers and educationalists define reading. For example, this can be seen in The National Literacy Trust's report on the *Read On. Get On* (ROGO) campaign, which begins with an attempt to conceptualise what is meant by the term 'reading', with a view to understanding what it means to be a reader at age 11. What is clear from the outset is that the concern here is not to understand what 'reading' is as such, but to define the concept of 'reading well'. This seems to assume that we share a definition of reading that is rooted in achieving mastery in reading skill. Fortunately, others have presented definitions that offer more of a balance between the concepts of skill and will; Clark and Teravainen (2017: 2) argue that reading skills can be categorised as 'a composite of two main cognitive processes: technical skills and comprehension skills' (p. 2), however, they stress that these cognitive processes alone do not define what reading is, as reading is a 'tripartite' of cognitive processes (decoding print and understanding text), affective processes (such as enjoying reading, confidence in reading, etc.) and behaviours (such as reading widely and frequently).

This definition suggests that teaching reading is a dynamic and complex process; it is argued that there is a need to teach skills so that children can decode print and make sense of what they are reading, but this must be situated in a context that continually encourages the 'will' to read. This forces us to consider the ways in which school discourses and curricula present definitions of reading. As authors, we recognise that we are writing this from

3

the vantage point of being twenty-first century British educational researchers, but it is simply not possible to talk about reading skills without facing the murky waters of 'phonics'. Over the years researchers have produced what McGuinness (2005: viii) has described as a 'huge and formidable' volume of studies which in various ways have tried to understand what helps children learn to read. As Lewis and Ellis (2006:2) point out, the fact that phonics is necessary in learning to read 'is not therefore at the heart of the current debate about the role of phonics', but rather the debate is now focused on what form of phonics should be taught, how much phonics should be taught, how often it should be taught and so forth. Phonics teaching must feature in the teaching of reading – but this raises serious questions about the extent to which phonics is allowed to play a central role in the how reading is *defined*. This is an important consideration and one that will be returned to at various points in this book.

There is no doubt that the schooling system is responsible for how many of us come to define what reading is, and how we perceive ourselves as readers; however, it is useful to look back at the ways in which reading practices have been perceived, and influenced, by socio-cultural and socio-historical factors over the years. Crucially, it is important to remember that reading is a human-made construct, which developed from the creation of the Phoenician alphabet during the twelfth century BC. While there are examples of people reading and writing throughout the decades to follow (see Styles, 1997 for example), concerns about one's ability to read did not originate much before the nineteenth century, because up to this point, being unable to read was regarded as a 'cultural norm' while being able to read was an 'exception to this norm' (Ramsey-Kurtz, 2007: 19).

Eric Havelock (1976) argues forcibly that as human beings have used oral speech for far longer than the comparatively late invention of alphabetic literacy, then this should take precedence within a definition. He states:

> The biological-historical fact is that *Homo sapiens* is a species which uses oral speech manufactured by the mouth, to communicate. This is his definition. He is not, by definition, a reader or a writer ... The habit of using written symbols to represent such speech is just a useful trick which has existed over too short a time to have been built into our genes.
>
> (Havelock, 1976, p. 12)

This view is supported by Galbraith (1997) who states that while some scholars make a sharp distinction between 'literacy' and 'orality', others take the view that the two cannot be easily separated. She herself argues that history teaches us to be cautious about making such distinctions because as recently as in late nineteenth-century Britain 'there was no clean break between orality and literacy, but instead a mix of the two within individual life cycles and in families and communities' (Galbraith, 1997, p. 3). Having closely examined the historical development of literacy, Harvey Graff takes this point further when he asserts his growing belief that literacy is *profoundly misunderstood* (italics in original) (1987, p. 17). He argues that many discussions about literacy flounder because 'they slight any effort to formulate consistent and realistic definitions of literacy, have little appreciation of the conceptual complications that the subject of literacy presents, and ignore – often grossly – the vital role of sociohistorical context' (1987, p. 17).

Even the briefest glance back into the socio-historical context is valuable in the introduction to this book, because it first reminds us that learning to read print is not part of 'natural' development but is something that humans have learned to do to communicate. Even if, just for the moment, we suspend concerns for promoting the 'will' to read, and just focus on skill, we see that reading is quite simply an ability to decode a human-made symbol and attach established sound and meaning to that symbol, or collection of symbols. What is more we know that young children start doing this from a very early age; way before they start school they may recognise icons, pictures, car badges, labels, shop signs, food packaging and so on. The point we are making here is that established definitions of reading, which focus on the decoding of print, are somewhat naïve, not just because they ignore the complexity of reading practices, but because they also fail to recognise that decoding print is just one of the ways in which humans have been bringing meaning to symbol for hundreds of years.

Yet there is no doubt that the ability to decode print remains central to many definitions of reading in society today, evident in the fact that there is serious international concern about children who fail to master this skill (Wheater et al., 2014; Mullis et al., 2011). This is not to say that this concern is unfounded. The 1970 British Cohort Study, for example, revealed 'a strong link between poor basic skills and disadvantaged life courses when participants were aged 34 (Bynner & Parsons 2006), with a disturbing picture of limited life chances, quality of life and social inclusion' (Levy et al., 2014). This same study, which followed 16,567 babies born in Great Britain in the period 5–11 April 1970, surveying them again in 1975, 1980, 1986, 1991, 1996 and 2000, found that improvement in reading skills for men was linked to increased home ownership and better employment prospects, while women were found to have experienced similar socio-economic benefits as their reading improved. What is more, these stronger prospects were also associated with reports of better mental health, physical health and general well-being (Bynner & Parsons, 2006).

Clearly, children who struggle to read print in text are at a disadvantage, but the question here is not so much about whether children should be taught to read in school (of course they should), but how definitions of reading that are embedded in schooling systems can impact on children's confidence and motivation for reading. Rachael's (author) previous research showed that the twelve young children in her study entered formal schooling with broad and sophisticated definitions of reading, and largely positive perceptions of themselves as readers; however, these constructions were threatened by the school discourse (Levy, 2011). In particular, it was evident that the ways in which reading scheme texts were perceived can have a profound effect on children's self-perceptions of reading and their wider relationships with text. This study revealed that many of these children came to believe that reading was, in fact, the decoding of print in reading scheme books, and being 'a reader' meant that a child had completed all of the stages in the scheme, and had thus been awarded the status of being 'on chapter books' (sometimes also referred to as being a 'free reader'). This has serious implications, as the stringent use of reading schemes in Reception was seen to actively discourage some children from reading and enforced negative self-perceptions of being a non-reader. Moreover, this study showed that by defining reading in this way, reading schemes did little to promote meaningful engagement with texts.

This is not to say that reading schemes do not have a place in teaching reading. However, bearing in mind the fact that reading print is a relatively 'new' human phenomenon, and the call to recognise the role of socio-historical context in defining what reading is, it is important to give serious consideration to the ways in which we have come to define what reading is. This is especially salient given the fact that constructions of reading are again changing in line with the development of digital technology. This raises all sorts of interesting questions about reading, starting with – what is 'text'? Traditionally, the word 'text' has been used to mean 'print'. For example, when we hear the phrase 'reading the text', it is often assumed that what is being read is the printed text, rather than another mode such as a visual image. But this raises further questions about text, namely what is 'a text'? Given that the word 'text' is commonly used to describe printed text, does *a* text have to contain print in order to be defined as 'a text'? And what does this mean for definitions of reading?

There is general acceptance that materials such as books, comics, magazines and newspapers are texts, even if there is little or even no printed text within (take children's wordless picture books as an example). However, advancements in technology mean that texts are becoming increasingly multimodal, meaning that they often use a combination of modes such as sound, image, moving image and so on. In 2003, Bearne argued forcibly that schools need to recognise these new forms of text in the curriculum, given that they are so evident in children's everyday lives – another point that we will return to later. The point we are making here is that the construction of 'text' is growing and now includes digital and screen texts, but this is not just about the physical media – it is about how these texts are accessed and understood. As Marsh and Singleton (2008, p. 1) point out, 'technology has always been part of literacy', be it a pencil, book, tablet, etc. However, as the literacy experience will inevitably have been influenced by the nature of the technology, literacy practices that have been mediated by digital technologies have been termed 'digital literacies' (Carrington & Robinson, 2009).

The extent to which definitions of the term 'digital literacy' should include the encoding and decoding of alphabetic print has been well debated by others. For example, Kress (2003) argues that 'literacy' refers to 'lettered representation', and as a result we need to find other ways to describe how digital texts are read, understood and used in terms of their broader symbolic representations. Merchant (2007, p. 121) agrees that the term 'digital literacy' relates to more than a general confidence in handling screen texts and should be orientated towards the 'study of written or symbolic representation that is mediated by new technology'. In other words, he appears to be arguing that the term 'digital literacy' can help to redefine conceptualisations of literacy as an ability to understand the many sign and symbol systems in existence within all manner of texts today, including the ways in which children make sense of texts within their home environments. Marsh (2005) also acknowledges that while the term 'points towards the ways in which lettered representation is being transformed and shaped by digitised technologies' (p. 4), she also recognises that 'there are distinct aspects of text analysis and production using new media' (p. 5) that cannot be described in the same way as the more traditional literacy practices.

This has implications for young children entering the school system today; as Albers, Frederick and Cowan (2009) point out, these children are not only regular users of a variety of digital and paper texts, but are developing the skills 'to help them make sense of complex multimodal features' (Levy & Marsh, 2011). What is more, given that many young children develop skills in reading digital texts before starting school (Marsh et al., 2005), they can face a challenge when entering formal schooling, as definitions of reading are dominated by the schooled discourse, which emphasises decoding print in books (and these are often reading scheme books). Again, it is not the purpose of this book to explore how children read in this multimodal world, but it is important to recognise from the outset that even though the school discourse promotes a singular and dominant definition of reading, it is an emerging construct that is shaped by social, historical and technological factors.

Together this raises two important points that rest at the heart of the study presented in this book. First, this book begins with the assumption that most of us want children to become confident, motivated and engaged readers, but in order to achieve this we must acknowledge that despite narrow schooled definitions of reading, it is a fluid construct. Given this understanding, the aim should surely be to support children in becoming confident in handling text in general – recognising that text now comes in many forms including paper and screen-based media. But how can this be achieved? This brings us to the second point, which relates to the need to step outside of the school context and focus on the home. In recent years researchers have become increasingly aware of the importance of the home environment in supporting children's development in literacy, but we still have a lot to learn. In 2005 McGuinness (2005; 410) argued that even though it had been known for over a decade that the home environment plays a critical role in supporting children's reading, 'reading researchers have failed to take into account the impact of the home environment', focusing instead on the children 'with reading problems, with the goal of finding out what's wrong with them'.

Over the last few decades, numerous studies have identified the home literacy environment as a key factor in children's language and literacy acquisition (Griffin & Morrison, 1997; Park, 2008; Brown et al., 2013). For example, there are a number of studies that support the view that parents who promote reading as a valuable and worthwhile activity are more likely to have children who are motivated to read for pleasure regardless of their social background (Baker & Scher, 2002). Further studies have found substantial differences in home literacy environments between children from high and low socio-economic families and used this to explain educational differences between children from these groups (Brooks-Gunn et al., 1996; Duncan et al., 1994); however, this is not to say that families in low socio-economic groups have 'poor' home literacy environments. Findings from the Organisation for Economic Co-operation and Development (OECD) (2002) indicate that while socio-economic status does have an impact on academic achievement, factors such as parental involvement with reading can in fact 'compensate' for low family income and educational background (see also Guthrie and Wigfield, 2000). In a similar vein, the Effective Provision of Pre-School Education (EPPE) Project, in an extensive study of early childhood provision, reported that 'for all children, the quality of the home learning environment is more important for intellectual and social development than parental occupation, education or income' (Sylva et al., 2004: ii).

So what is meant by a 'quality' home literacy environment? This is not at all straightforward to answer. As we have already established, reading is a shifting construct, shaped by social, cultural and historical factors, so it is to be expected that families will have developed their own literacy practices, which include unique and individual perceptions of reading and engagement with text. Yet we also know that the school discourse not only presents a narrow and static definition of reading, which is governed by a focus on accurately decoding print in books, but that this discourse is dominant in society. This creates something of a tension for the study of reading with young children in families; however, the first step in addressing this tension is to recognise that it exists.

We know that there are a number of benefits associated with reading with young children. For example, it has now been well documented that children who are read to regularly in the preschool years are more likely to learn language faster, enter school with a larger vocabulary and become more 'successful' readers at school (Bus et al., 1995; Mol et al., 2008). The purpose of this book is to explore family reading practices, and the barriers and motivations to reading with young children in homes, with a view to supporting more families in reading with their children. However, this book is not about helping families to prepare their children for school. Rather this book is about *understanding* what families do in terms of reading with their children. It is about understanding what reading means to them, why they read, how they read and what influences reading activity. Given that further study has stressed the importance of understanding and valuing the literacy practices in the home and building on existing *funds of knowledge* within (Moll et al., 1995; Reese & Gallimore, 2000), this book seeks to understand the ways in which reading fits within the context of everyday life and family practices. It should be stressed at this point that this book will make regular reference to 'parents'; however, it is intended that the term is used broadly and includes any adults in the child's home, or indeed their lives, who have responsibility for care-giving.

Reading with young children can of course take on many forms and mean different things, but it generally includes sharing a text with a child. For this reason, the term 'shared reading' will appear regularly in this book. The next section takes a specific look at the term 'shared reading', exploring how it has been perceived in the literature, and what is generally meant by the term.

What is 'shared reading'?

Despite the fact that shared reading has been fairly well researched, and this is discussed in more detail in Chapter 2, it is surprisingly difficult to locate a definition for the term in the literature. Given the discussion above, we take the view that shared reading describes an activity where a child is engaged in focusing on a text with another person (usually an adult) for a sustained period of time. We agree with Yuill and Martin (2016: 2) who argue that the joint attention on a text 'fundamentally involves the shared construction of meaning', suggesting that an element of shared understanding is created by the event. As discussed in the previous section, young children now engage with a variety of texts that include digital and multimodal formats (Marsh et al., 2005; Carrington & Robinson, 2009), meaning that family shared reading may now centre on technological devices such as laptops, mobiles and tablets (Aliagas & Margallo, 2016). It is apparent that the literature also suggests that much of the reading that takes place between young children and their parents still involves the use of books (Dickinson, 2001; Denny et al., 2010). For this reason, shared reading is often described in the literature as 'shared book reading' (SBR), 'joint book reading' or 'parent–child book reading' (Kucirkova et al., 2018). Even though many of the parents in this present study spoke largely about books, we feel it is important to use the word 'text' rather than book in defining shared reading activity.

9

Shared reading can be sub-divided into two quite different activities; reading to/with a child and listening to a child read. Both types of shared reading have their advantages, with Martin-Chang and Gould (2012: 871) arguing that they are both 'fundamentally sound activities that create prospects for developing literacy appreciation and reading skill'; however, they tend to be born from different priorities and offer different opportunities for fostering literacy development. For example, 'literacy appreciation', which includes factors such as positive attitudes about reading, tends to be prioritised when adults are reading to children, while 'skill improvement' is more likely to be the focus of attention when children are reading to adults (Martin-Chang & Gould, 2012: 855). Similarly, de Jong, Mol and Bus (2009) and Mol, Bus, de Jong and Smeets (2008) also argued that there are likely to be positive, but different consequences associated with shared book reading depending on whether children are listening to a story or reading a text to someone else.

Although there are obvious links between these two different types of shared reading, this book is primarily concerned with reading to/with children, rather than listening to children read. One reason for this is that as children progress through their early years in school, the priority often seems to shift from reading to children, to listening to children read. As Wolfendale stated in 1985, the 'time-honoured means of parents helping their children learn to read is by listening to them reading' (35), and indeed most schools continue to ask parents to listen to their children read, especially in the early years, though it should be acknowledged that many schools also encourage parents to read to their children. But there is a shift in perception of value. It is often regarded as more important that children 'practice' their reading as often as possible, as this is the 'real work' of early years education, while reading to children is seen as being altogether more inconsequential. Yet there is substantial evidence to show that there are significant benefits in adults reading to children in their homes. For example, it has been recognised that sharing books with children facilitates a particular kind of talk because speech, during book-reading, is more complex than during caretaking or play (Snow, 1994). In other words, it is the talk that surrounds shared reading activity that is so valuable, as it provides opportunities for parent and child to talk about all kinds of concepts that may not have otherwise arisen. Snow (1994) summarises this nicely when she states that in shared reading the book becomes

> ... a microenvironment within which certain kinds of events are likely to occur, events like: learning new words, asking why questions, learning scientific facts, or seeing connections between one's own life and others' lives ... the talk is the site of the learning; the book-reading is important because it is the site of the talk.
>
> (Snow, 1994:271)

Talk occurring between parent and child during shared reading activity is often more complex, in terms of sentence structure and vocabulary, than talk which happens during other activities such as free play, sharing meals and so on. This was evidenced by Fletcher and Reese (2005) in relation to picture book reading with children under the age of three. However, this is not just about the structure of language during shared reading activity. The text becomes a focal site of engagement for parent and child, offering numerous opportunities to talk about issues, experiences, events, concerns, identities and so on. It should also be noted that the text which is central to this activity may well be a book (in paper or screen format), but it could also be any other artefact such as a picture or photograph.

While the specific content of the talk will be dependent on the individual child, parent and text, the point to recognise is that shared reading offers unique possibilities for talk that are highly beneficial. This appears to be related to the kind of interaction that occurs between parent and child during shared reading activity, which can be described as *joint attention* (JA). 'Joint attention' describes a situation where parents and children are jointly fixated on a particular object and coordinate visual attention together. Studies into child development have suggested that joint attention has less to do with a child following an adults' gaze but occurs when the gaze of both parties is coordinated and jointly focused on the object (Yu & Smith, 2007; Baldwin & Moses, 1996). This is critical when considering shared reading activity as the mutual focus on a text fosters joint attention between parent and child. This is important because further studies have shown that language acquisition is facilitated by joint parent–child attention, given that joint attention between parent and child is itself known to be a predictor of children's language skills (Kucirkova et al., 2018; Karrass et al., 2002).

Shared reading clearly has language benefits for young children; however, these are not the only advantages. Further study has shown that shared reading can facilitate a number of social and emotional benefits including the fact that it can enhance the relationship between parent and child. This is discussed next.

Social and emotional benefits in shared reading

There is much to suggest that parents and children enjoy shared reading. For example, in the opening pages of her book *Help Your Child Love Reading*, David (2014) recalls her own experiences in reading with her son, saying 'I can honestly say that reading to and with him is one of the most joyful and pleasurable things we do together'. While research has tended to focus more attention on the language benefits of shared reading, rather than the socio-emotional advantages, it is not hard to find evidence of the pleasure that can be found in shared reading, for both parents and children. For example, Scher and Baker (1996) found that only 4% of their socially and culturally diverse sample of parents reported that their first-grade children did not like having someone read to them, suggesting that this is something that children generally enjoy. Similarly, studies have also suggested that parents often value the affective dimensions of shared reading; for example, in their study of 119 parents, Audet et al. (2008) found that these parents reported that their goals for shared reading included bonding with their child, soothing their child and enjoying books, together with the more 'educational' goals to stimulate development and foster reading.

Research with babies and very young children has also shed light on the affective benefits of shared reading activity. Evaluating a book programme for mothers and their seven-month-old babies, Hardman and Jones (1999) noted that interactions around books with these young children were social rituals providing opportunities for social interaction and physical proximity. As there was a lack of emphasis on following a storyline at this early age, their observations suggested that the book facilitated social interaction between parent and child, which included the child touching, chewing and looking at the book. As a consequence, the value of the activity appeared to be in enabling social interaction and close contact, rather than developing skills in reading as such.

Shared reading can be a highly enjoyable activity, facilitating closeness and strengthening the relationship between parent and child. While this is a valuable aim in its own right, research also indicates that the stronger the affective-emotional relationship during shared reading, the more likely the language benefits for the child. This was seen in Britto et al.'s (2006) study of mothers reading to their children, which concluded that a mother's praise and enthusiasm during shared reading encouraged the child's verbal participation. Similarly, other research has suggested that a strong affective-emotional climate encourages the child to focus attention on the text and show enthusiasm for the reading experience. Children in these situations were also more likely to co-operate with the mother's requests, which in turn led to more frequent shared reading activities (Bus et al., 1997; Leseman & de Jong, 1998). There are also suggestions in the literature that secure attachments between parents and children are associated with activities such as shared reading (Frosch et al., 2001); however, given that many of these studies tend to take a very binary view of attachment we do feel that caution is needed in making claims about the relationship between shared reading and parent–child 'attachment'.

That said, when we bring this all together, we can see that shared reading has a number of benefits for both parent and child; while there is much to indicate that shared reading promotes language development in children, it also provides an opportunity for parent and child to enjoy time together and develop their relationship. What is more, the literature also suggests that the relationship between parent and child can influence the shared reading experience, with securely attached children being more likely to experience enthusiastic and focused shared reading activity. This may not be terribly surprising in itself, as it stands to reason that difficulties in the relationship between parent and child will likely be reflected in the activities that they share. However, given the importance of shared reading in terms of language development, and the need to encourage the activity in children's homes, this does remind us that the relational aspects of shared reading must be acknowledged in research to understand how it operates in families.

Researching shared reading

We know that shared reading is good for children, with many of the benefits being discussed in this introduction. We also know that not all children are engaged in shared reading activity in their own homes (Britto et al., 2002). This suggests a need to understand the factors that both encourage and prevent parents from reading with their children, in an attempt to find ways in which to support more parents in reading with their children. But we need to be careful. We also know that many reading interventions with families simply do not work (Justice et al., 2015), often because the intervention has failed to acknowledge the socio-cultural dynamic of the individual family. This suggests a need to understand what families do and how shared reading fits, or not, within the context of their everyday family lives.

So far, much of the research into shared reading has tended to focus on how the activity promotes literacy development (Bus et al., 2007; Mol et al., 2008) or what parents do during the activity to foster this development (Price et al., 2009; Baker et al., 2001). Far fewer studies have attempted to understand what parents think about shared reading and explore the barriers to engaging in the activity. Among those that have, such as Harris et al. (2007), parents have been restricted to selecting from a set of fixed responses, which may not measure the things that are most relevant to them. Lin et al. (2015) considered a broader range of barriers to reading with children, showing that mothers are more likely to report child-centred barriers than any other type; however, the authors acknowledged the limitations of restricting the barriers that parents could report. They called for interview methods to be used to identify additional factors that prevent parents from reading with their children. The study presented in this book addresses this, by enabling parents to express in their own way how shared reading is perceived in their homes and how it fits, or does not fit, within everyday family life.

Overview of the book

Having introduced the concept of shared reading in this chapter, and explained our justification for focusing on this, the next chapter (Chapter 2) takes a step back and explores how the overall concept of 'reading' can be understood when we explore it from a sociological perspective. We look at how the home and school contexts are responsible for the socialisation of reading, concluding that reading is a value-laden activity, embedded in discourses of power and shaped by systems and beliefs. Chapter 3 returns to a focus on shared reading, exploring how factors such as culture and ethnicity, as well as social factors, are linked with shared reading in families. This chapter also shows how shared reading is a highly complex phenomenon, influenced by social and cultural structures as well as the unique features of everyday family life.

Chapter 4 moves to the research that is presented in this book. We introduce the study and explain the methods that were used to conduct the research. We focus attention on the process of developing the in-depth interviews which allowed us to gain an insight into the lives of our participants. Chapters 5 to 8 present a detailed overview of what we learned from talking to the parents in our study. Chapter 5 demonstrates how reading was an everyday practice for many of the families in this study; we show how these families used shared reading to structure and manage daily life as well as display aspects of 'being a family'. Building on this, Chapter 6 explores parents' motivation for reading, focusing on the link between enjoyment and feedback within the activity and showing how these factors are part of a reciprocal cycle that develops within shared reading relationships. Chapter 7 turns to potential barriers to shared reading, demonstrating that just as shared reading can happen for many different reasons, there are a number of factors that can inhibit or prevent the practice from taking place. By getting to know the families in this study we grew to understand how immensely important it is for parent and child to enjoy the activity, suggesting that it is not enough for practitioners to simply encourage parents to read with their children, but they must support parents in finding ways to make the activity enjoyable for all. Chapter 8 concludes this section of the book by exploring the parents' own relationships with reading and the ways in which this linked with shared reading practices with their children. This chapter shows how for some of the parents in this study, shared reading with their children had a positive impact on their own relationships with reading which they both recognised and valued.

The final two chapters of the book turn to the implications of this study for practitioners working with families. By reflecting on the data presented in Chapters 5 to 8, we present a new definition for shared reading in homes that is characterised by 'The Four T's' of text, talk, time and togetherness. Chapter 9 examines how this understanding, and indeed the findings presented throughout this book, can be used by practitioners to support their work with families. Chapter 10 brings the book to a conclusion by demonstrating how shared reading in the home offers a very different definition of reading to that of the school, which, we argue, can inhibit shared reading practices and in some cases stifle children's engagement with reading altogether. By making this comparison transparent, we conclude this book by showing why it is important for parents to continue shared reading practices after their children start school, and into the future for as long as they can.

2

SOCIOLOGICAL PERSPECTIVES ON READING

Introduction

Reading is an everyday practice. In fact, it is very hard to get through daily life without having to read something in one way or another. Like many other features of everyday life, it is easy for many of us to take the process for granted and see it from a 'common sense' perspective; what this means is that we may assume that we share a uniform view of what reading is, how we all read and what its purpose is. However, as highlighted in Chapter 1, reading is in fact a highly complex activity, moulded by socio-historical factors and changing textual landscapes. This means that reading, as a concept, is not static, but is a fluid and developing construct. Yet educational and social discourses are ever present, influencing the ways in which values permeate dominant views about reading. For this reason, it is important to understand how values influence perceptions of reading if we are to support more children and families in reading in the home.

Many of the values attached to reading can be seen in the context of everyday life. Take for example the headlines that decry the culling of libraries as one of the many regrettable outcomes of austerity measures imposed on local councils (Swaffield, 2017); or the fact that when books are adapted for television or cinema, the result is invariably compared to the original book, and often unfavourably so (Hutcheon, 2006). These examples demonstrate some of the ways in which people express their views about reading; however, you don't need to look very deeply to see how values are embedded within. Reading – and we are talking here about reading books – is often portrayed as a cherished activity, something to be prized above other pursuits. However, if reading books is a respected endeavour, what does this mean for those who do not read books? This becomes evident when we consider how attitudes towards literacy skill sit in comparison with numeracy skills. This is summarised in the words of Jennifer Ouellette (2010), in her exploration of calculus, when she said:

I think scientists have a valid point when they bemoan the fact that it's socially acceptable in our culture to be utterly ignorant of math, whereas it is a shameful thing to be illiterate.

(2010: 13)

It should be noted that many authors are not comfortable with the word 'illiteracy' as it is rare for a person to have no literacy; this can be seen in the work of Barton (2007) who argues that the term 'low levels of literacy' is often more accurate when describing a person who struggles with literacy skill. However, the point that is being made in Ouellette's quote is still important as society does cast judgement on those who are deemed to have low levels of literacy skill, in comparison with other curriculum subjects such as mathematics, scientific understanding and so on. As raised in the Introduction, we know that children and adults who do not master basic skills in reading are at a disadvantage (Bynner & Parsons, 2006), and as a result the education system is deeply concerned about supporting children's reading. However, Ouellette's point is not so much to do with the desire to teach children to read but is recognising that reading is immersed in values. This has substantial implications for children who are learning to read.

This is compounded by the perceived capital associated with reading, whether for pleasurable or informative motivations, in relation to the texts themselves. For example, books and comics hold very different notions of worth (Meskin, 2011); books are often aligned with notions of education (consider how the term 'bookish' is used to describe studious children) while comics are more often associated with entertainment. As Levy et al. (2014) suggest, 'literacy is connected with respectability, and certain forms of text and reading material are considered by some to have more currency than others' (35). Take for example one participant in the research presented in this book who told us that she is 'not a reader' but does occasionally read autobiographies. This suggests that certain literature is considered to be less important, or less worthwhile than others. In this instance we can only assume that the participant was suggesting that while novels were aligned with 'real reading', autobiographies were not, but this is speculative.

What is clear is that reading is deeply embedded in constructions of class, worth and value; therefore one of the purposes of this chapter is to delve into these notions by examining reading from a sociological perspective. By applying a sociological lens, we can explore the ways in which reading functions as a social practice. We begin this chapter by exploring what is meant by the term 'socialisation' before moving on to a discussion about the specific ways in which the discourses of home and school can impact on how children come to define reading and engage with the activity. Building on this, we then draw from some sociological studies to explore reading as a family practice and understand how families may use reading activity to display aspects of their family life.

Agents of socialisation

The term 'socialisation' refers to the process by which individuals acquire the skills to fit into, and adhere to, society's expectations; in other words, it is 'the process of becoming social, the process of growing up and getting to know the world' (James, 2013: 16). Given that socialisation is often about getting to know the world within which we live, it is not surprising that it is commonly associated with childhood; however, it is in fact a lifelong process as individuals become assimilated into different phases of the life course or societies. The sociologist Talcott Parsons (1951) drew attention to the functional aspects of society, asserting that the continuity of society relied upon the socialisation of children in order to replicate the social order. This idea has been explored by numerous scholars over the years and is of particular interest to philosophers, many of whom have argued that a main function of education is to produce 'good citizens' who then contribute towards a 'good society' and a 'good life'. For example, Carr and Harnett (1996: 30) argue that one cannot separate 'political philosophy' from 'educational philosophy' as state education in particular can be regarded as politically motivated to reproduce the kind of citizens that are 'useful' to society and the development of a strong economy.

Social 'norms' exist in a whole variety of contexts and the perpetuation of these allow for certain structures to be reproduced within society. Children are of course heavily influenced by a number of factors originating from domains such as their homes, families, schools, religious communities and the media. Each of these have been described as 'agents of socialisation' and each been considered to play a particular role in the reproduction of knowledge, views, values, skills and so on. How children are socialised by the various domains within which they are situated, and the influence this has on their lives, is clearly a complex phenomenon. Our understanding of this can be traced back to the influential work of Bronfenbrenner, a psychologist who sought to understand how various external influences affect the family, and the development of children within families. His ecological systems theory identifies five environmental systems within which a young person interacts, showing how young people's development is affected by the 'bigger picture' (Bronfenbrenner, 1979; 1986; 1990). For example, the *macrosystem* acknowledges the wider influences of society including the attitudes and ideology of a culture, while the *microsystem* includes factors such as family, peers and school. However, Bronfenbrenner then extends this to the *mesosystem*, which recognises the ways in which the relationships between these factors, whichever system they are situated in, can have an influence on the child. For example Bronfenbrenner (1986: 2) raises the point that 'events at home can affect a child's progress in school, and vice versa'. While this may appear obvious, research that has been designed to identify the influences operating in both directions has been relatively recent. In other words, Bronfenbrenner is claiming that the identification of the mesosystem has allowed researchers to understand the ways in which school experiences affect the behaviour of children and parents in the home, as well as the influence of the family on children's performance and behaviour in school.

This is an important consideration in the quest to understand reading from a sociological perspective, as it highlights the need to recognise directionality within the different domains that influence perceptions of reading. Given that institutions such as schools and homes play a major role in the structure of children's lives and are particularly central in influencing children's perceptions of reading, we now look specifically at the ways in which these two domains, and the conversation between these domains, can influence perceptions of reading.

Schools and the socialisation of reading

It is a commonly held belief that one of the prime functions of early childhood education is to teach children how to read. What is more, it is also widely acknowledged that teaching phonics is central to this process; however, considerable controversy has existed for years regarding 'the best way' to teach reading and the role of phonics teaching within this. Debates became particularly heated throughout the 1970s and 1980s (see Moya Cove (2006) for an outline of the development of phonics teaching during this time), and debates concerning the teaching of phonics have become just as volatile in more recent years. Take, for example, Johnston and Watson's research evidence from Clackmannanshire (SOEID, 1998), which claimed that children being taught to read using synthetic phonics achieved better results than those taught using analytic phonics. This resulted in a national review of the teaching of phonics in England, culminating in the publication of the Rose Report (DfES, 2005), which concluded that 'the case for systematic phonic work is overwhelming and much strengthened by a synthetic approach' (DfES, 2006: 20). The impact of this has resonated to this day. For example, a recent study with experienced graduate level early years practitioners found that these educators believed that formally 'teaching' systematic synthetic phonics (SSP) to two-year olds was 'best practice' in preparing them for school (Boardman, 2019). In fact, these early years educators were actually investing in expensive SSP programmes to use with children under the age of three, as they did not feel they had any other resources to support the reading development of their children.

This shows that phonics teaching, and SSP in particular, has had a major influence on constructions of 'reading' and conceptualisations of what it means to be 'a reader'. Kathy Hall (2006) helps us to understand how this has come about, arguing that these kinds of beliefs originate from differences in how people view knowledge. If an individual sees knowledge as something that is 'fixed', 'certain' and detached from the knower, then literacy becomes viewed as 'an individual and linear accomplishment, made up of a discrete set of skills, like phonics, fluency and comprehension' (Hall, 2006: 10). The impact of this is that teaching reading is then likely to be viewed as a something that is uniform, rigid and prescribed. As discussed above, the fact that some early-year educators believe that it is in the best interests of young children to introduce them to SSP before they are three years of age is testament to this view. But what if this was *not* how we view knowledge? What if knowledge – and this includes knowledge about the alphabet – is seen as something that is active, and learners are seen as being what Hall describes as 'intentional beings whose wider knowledge, feelings, experiences and identities constantly filter their understanding'? Then teaching reading becomes a process which extends beyond asking whether children 'can read' and involves broader questions about what learners 'do' with their reading, and how they engage with it.

What becomes clear from this discussion is that the teaching of reading in school not only has an impact on *how* children read, but on children's perceptions of what reading is and what it means to be *a reader*. To put this another way, when schools display a heavy emphasis on the teaching of phonics and fail to acknowledge what children 'do' with their reading, then this can have an impact on how children (and indeed their parents) come to define reading within the context of the school discourse. What is more, this can have a serious impact on young children's perceptions of themselves as readers from their earliest days in school.

This was explored in detail by one of the authors of this book (Rachael), who followed two parallel cohorts of six children over the course of one complete academic year, in order to understand children's perceptions of reading at the time of entry into the formal education system (Levy, 2011). Rachael followed the first cohort from Nursery into Reception, and the second from Reception into Year One. For purposes of clarity, as this study was conducted in England, this meant that the Nursery children were aged 3–4 years and the Reception children were aged 4–5 years. Reception, while still part of the *Foundation Stage*, is actually the first year of compulsory schooling, and is the year in which children generally begin the formal process of learning to read in the UK.

While some interviews were conducted in the children's homes, most of the data were collected at school and involved the use of two main activities: the 'Charlie Chick' interview and the 'Small World Play' activity. The first research activity used a glove puppet (Charlie Chick) to mediate discussions between the researcher and the child. The children were told that the puppet knew very little about school but wanted to learn about it. In this respect the children were encouraged to take up the role of 'expert' and explain their understandings of concepts to Charlie Chick. For example, the puppet asked the children to show him what 'reading' is, as well as answer questions such as, 'What is reading?', 'How do you learn to read?' and 'What does it mean if you can't read?' The 'Small World Play' activity was designed to encourage a dialogue between child and researcher, using a variety of 'home-scenario' artefacts to facilitate a play-orientated research conversation. The scenario scene included furniture (e.g. tables and chairs), a computer and a television as well as a family of dolls. Using the scenario as a basis for role-play, the children were encouraged to talk about the different kinds of activities the family would engage with in their home, including the reading of screen and paper-based texts.

This study found that the nursery children owned broader constructions of 'reading' than the Reception children and were therefore more likely to include strategies such as picture-reading within their own definition of reading. Yet, once the children entered Reception, many of these valuable constructions of reading were overridden by the dominance of the school discourse on reading. The study concluded:

> Despite the fact that many of the children were clearly learning much about ways in which to find meaning from texts, as well as developing confidence and motivations for reading through the context of their own home discourse, the children quickly came to believe that 'real' reading was situated in the decoding of print in books. As a consequence, many of the children in this study came to believe that they were 'non-readers' or 'poor readers' from their earliest years in school, because they believed they were unable to fulfil the demands of the school discourse in reading.
>
> (Levy, 2011: 63)

What is more, this study revealed that many of these children came to perceive 'success' in reading as strongly related to achievement within their reading scheme (Levy, 2009a). Also known as 'basal readers', a reading scheme is a series of levelled books that gradually increase in length and complexity in terms of vocabulary, sentence length and sentence structure. The children in this study widely reported a belief that the reading scheme existed to *teach* them to read; this meant that many of the children did not believe that they were 'readers' until they had completed all of the stages in the reading scheme and were awarded the position of being 'on chapter books' or being 'a free reader'. What this study has shown is that despite the best of intentions, schools can socialise children from their earliest years into adopting an accepted definition of reading. While this may not have a detrimental effect on all children, for some it can result in a developing belief that they 'not readers' because they have not yet learned how to fulfil the requirements of the school discourse regarding achievement in reading.

21

While this research raised real concerns about the impact of the school discourse on children's constructions of reading, it is important to remember that children do not just learn to read at school. Perceptions of reading are formed in both the school and the home. What is more, although the concept of socialisation has historically cast children as passive recipients within the process – therefore viewing the process as something being done *to* children, it is becoming increasingly recognised that children are key social actors in the school, home and beyond (James, 2013) and are fully involved in making social connections (Denzin, 1977). For example, James (2013) makes a compelling case for a child-centred theorisation of socialisation, which acknowledges that 'it is not that "the family" can be said to socialise the child in one way or another as traditional socialisation would have it; rather, it is children who, by living with their family, come to learn about, reflect on and even help shape its particular values, attitudes and roles' (72). Given this understanding, we now turn to look at the home and family in the socialisation of reading.

Homes and the socialisation of reading

We know that a child's home environment is a critical factor in their educational journey, something that has been recognised by sociologists for a number of years now (Douglas, 1964; Bourdieu, 1992). Contemporary research has continued to suggest a relationship between children's academic achievement and the extent to which parents are involved in their education, with greater involvement considered congruent with academic attainment (Morgan et al., 2009). While there remains much concern about the ways in which schools do, or do not engage successfully with parents, recognition of the value of the home is now starting to permeate educational policy (McNamara et al., 2000; Reay, 2004). This has resulted in the publication of a number of guides available for schools on how to involve parents and families in children's schooling (e.g. Henderson et al., 2007; Epstein et al., 2008), most of which emphasise the benefits for children's learning when parents and families are involved (Whalley, 2007; Harris et al., 2009).

Schools and educational organisations are indeed starting to recognise that there is much to be gained from working in partnership with parents, but this generally means that schools want parents to support their work, rather than taking time to understand what parents are already doing at home. This is particularly evident in relation to literacy, with many schools encouraging parents to engage in literacy activity that will support the literacy curriculum in schools. It is true to say that organisations such as The National Literacy Trust (2006) have stated that 'parents are one of the most important literacy teachers' and urge schools to 'capitalise on and encourage reading that is done at home' (Clark & Rumbold, 2006); however, there is little attempt being made to *understand* how literacy is constructed, developed and practiced in homes, and the impact of this on how children perceive reading.

Yet the home environment is incredibly influential in the development of children's literate identities. For example, language socialisation studies have shown the powerful ways in which children are socialised in the home to develop social identities regarding features such as religion, gender, learning disability and authority (Goodwin, 1990; Gutierrez & Stone, 1997; Mehan, 1996). Studies have also shown how children arrive at school with their own unique reading histories, which they have learned socially and culturally from their families and communities (Minns, 1990; Levy, 2008, 2009b). This was also evidenced with great clarity in the iconic work of Heath (1982, 1983), which is discussed in more detail in the next chapter.

Given that this book is primarily concerned with understanding the ways in which shared reading practices operate in families with young children, the role of families in promoting children's engagement with reading is a critical avenue for exploration. However, in order to take this discussion further, it is useful to consider some of the sociological literature that has focused on family practices more broadly, and the ways in which families display these practices in order to help us conceptualise reading as a family practice.

Understanding reading as family practice and display

When one considers the socialisation of reading, and reading as a social practice, the role of the family is paramount. As discussed above, there is no shortage of evidence to suggest that the home and family are crucial in supporting children's literacy, including their reading. The home plays a significant role in how children come to view reading, given that literacy is 'learned socially and culturally within their family and community and that the types of literacy experience children encounter differ according to families' social and cultural practices' (Morgan et al., 2009: 168). However, if we are to truly understand the relationship between the home and children's literacy learning, then we perhaps need to move away from the question 'How is reading developed within the family?' towards the question 'What does reading do for the construct of family practices?' In other words, this is not just about understanding what families do in terms of reading but involves an exploration which seeks to understand what reading does for families. But before any discussion about family practices can take place, we need to consider how the term 'family' is perceived and used, and the implications of this definition.

What is 'family'?

Despite being such an everyday familiar term, it is hard to define the construct of 'family'. Dictionary definitions are broad and speak of 'social units consisting of parents and their children', 'the spouse and children of a person' and 'a household under one head', which may include 'parents, children and servants' (dictionary.com accessed 24 May 2019). Clearly these definitions do little to demonstrate the complexity of 'the family', especially within modern society; Finch (2007: 67), drawing on the work of Williams' (2004) '*Rethinking Families*', pointed out that research in recent years has emphasised 'the essential diversity of family composition and the fluidity of family relationships', meaning that it has become increasingly difficult to ascertain what is meant by the term 'my family'.

In recent years, studies into family life have moved away from viewing the family as a structure, and instead define family in terms of what they 'do' rather than what they 'are'. Morgan (1996) was particularly influential in shifting sociological analysis away from the structural elements of 'being' a family, towards 'understanding families as sets of activities which take on a particular meaning, associated with family, at a given point in time' (Finch, 2007: 66). In other words, Morgan is arguing that 'family' is a 'facet of social life' and is therefore represented by 'a quality' rather than 'a thing' (Morgan, 1996: 186). Similarly, Finch (2007: 66) makes the point that 'family does not equate to household', arguing that it is more helpful to focus on the relational aspects of 'the family', rather than try to define *who* the family is. The word 'family' therefore acts as a verb (something that we '*do*'), rather than operating as a noun (something that we '*are*').

This lens has illuminated how families continue to operate in diverse and challenging circumstances. For example, the concept has yielded rich insights into how families continue to 'be family' when a family member is dying (Ellis, 2013), has dementia (Hall & Sikes, 2016) or is in prison (Jardine, 2017). Together this encapsulates the notion of 'family practices', which Morgan (1996) describes as 'often little fragments of daily life which are part of the normal taken-for-granted existence of practitioners [i.e. family members]' (p. 190). This focus on what families do suggests that the concept of 'family' can be viewed in terms of daily practice and everyday activity; however, this is not without contention. It is also well known that ways of 'doing' family are socially and culturally situated (Morgan, 1996; Williams, 2004) and are embedded in discourses power (Ren & Hu, 2011). What this means is that certain family practices may be privileged above others. In order to understand this further, Finch (2007) went on to develop the notion of 'family display', which draws attention to the idea that family activities are not just performed but are also *seen* to be performed.

Displaying 'family'

When we consider the notion of family display, with the emphasis on how family activities are *seen* to be performed, this raises the question of audience – who is the audience to this performance? The fact that Finch

24

(2007) argues convincingly that 'family display' exists because it provides evidence to its own members, as well as to outsiders, that individuals are 'doing' family and reaffirming relationships to one another, suggests that the audience may be external to the family but may well be the family itself. To put it simply, family activities may be displayed as a way of saying, in Finch's words, 'this is my family and it works' (2007: 73). This is pertinent when we consider that parenting can be experienced and constructed as something of a moral endeavour (Shirani et al., 2012) and that there can be a pressure to not only *be* a 'good' parent, but to also be *seen* to be a good parent.

This was evident in a study of middle-class mothers' preparation of lunchboxes for their children (Harman & Capellini, 2015). Having researched eleven mothers from a primary school in England, Harman and Cappellini (2015) found that in the preparation of lunchboxes for their children to take to school, these mothers were 'displaying, to themselves as well as external audiences (such as school-teachers and lunchtime supervisors, the researchers) that they are competent, caring mothers' (776). Care was taken to ensure that the lunch they prepared was not only crafted to accommodate the individual requests of their children but displayed the characteristics of a 'proper' lunchbox, meaning that it had to meet accepted standards of being relatively 'healthy' and nutritionally balanced. Harman and Cappellini concluded that this showed that despite being part of a relatively hegemonic group of white middle-class mothers, anxiety about the display of their mothering meant that these women 'felt under scrutiny and potentially under attack' (Harman & Cappellini, 2015: 778). Keeping with the theme of food, James and Curtis (2010: 1173) reported that they too found evidence of parents wishing to display that they were 'doing family properly' in the meals they prepared for their children, the display of having 'family meals' together and even in the food that was ordered when families ate together outside of the home. James and Curtis argue that as their research took place during a time of substantial concern about healthy eating and childhood obesity, and when issues about 'poor parenting' were also high on the political agenda, so it was probably no coincidence that their participants' individual narratives reflected 'the current political climate of widespread concern about children's diets, childhood obesity and parental responsibility for children's food choice'.

These studies show how aspects of family life can demonstrate to an audience that their family practices reflect the substance of 'good parenting'. Of course, how one comes to make a judgement about what constitutes 'good parenting' is highly questionable, but what we do know is that these perceptions are steeped in discourses of power and control and are closely related to constructions of a social norm. This is clearly an issue for all parents; however, it is fair to say that normative constructions of parenting still tend to place a greater emphasis on mothers than fathers.

In the twenty-first century, gendered aspects of parenting continue to play out, with mothers occupying a prominent role in a society that remains, despite diversification, fundamentally rooted in the male breadwinner/female carer model (Vincent, 2017). As Vincent (2017) suggests 'parent is, in practice, rarely the gender-neutral term that it appears to be … parenting responsibilities still fall most heavily upon women, and particularly upon working-class women' (541). In appraisals of research on family literacy programmes, Nutbrown and colleagues note that 'parent' and 'mother' are used almost interchangeably (Morgan et al., 2009). Accounts of father's involvement in childcare (Vincent, 2017) describe a multitude of approaches to parenting (as can be applied to motherhood of course); for example, some were unwilling to fully participate in childcare and some described a reluctance among mothers to relinquish control over a role that they valued; however, Vincent et al. (2017) concluded that fathers are increasingly choosing to be more involved in the daily care of their children (Vincent, 2017). This suggests that fathers, as a group, may have some element of choice in the extent to which their parenting is displayed to others.

There is no shortage of literature showing how constructions of gender continue to place a particular burden on women regarding the ways in which aspects of parenting are displayed and judged by society (Fine, 2010; Aveling, 2002). To illustrate, judgements about what constitutes 'good mothering' can begin from the moment a pregnancy is confirmed (if not before) and may include a focus on factors such as the mother's diet, her weight, her daily habits and activities, her plans for feeding her baby and her intention to work after the baby is born. In other words, pregnancy results in women's motherhood being on display, and therefore judged, well before their children are even born. Once the child has arrived, it is not a surprise to see that much of the literature on feeding children is focused on mothers as in Harman and Capellini's (2015) research cited above, which resulted in these mothers reporting that they felt 'under scrutiny and potentially under attack' (Harman & Cappellini, 2015: 778). As Levy (2016) pointed out in her historical reflection into gendered constructions, things have not changed over the years as much as we would hope, as social norms continue to dictate that home and children remain primarily the woman's responsibility. This is evident in the fact that 'mums still "go to Iceland" (this is a tag-line from a commercial for the British supermarket chain "Iceland") in order produce satisfying meals that are compatible with a family budget, while the purchase of Kentucky Fried Chicken still allows mums to have "a night off" (a catch-phrase in another British commercial)' (Levy, 2016: 287).

While it is important that we do not forget that concerns about displaying 'good parenting' often weigh more heavily on mothers, it would be wrong to suggest that fathers do not feel these concerns too. For example, McKeown (2001: 3) argues that fathers are now 'being judged against changing expectations of what it is to be a good father', going on to define the 'good'

26

(4) father as one who is emotionally involved with his child as well as being a provider. Clearly, concerns about displaying family practices as a mark of 'good parenting' is something that affects all parents, and this may be linked to societal constructions of gender and the judgements which are embedded within. Of course, displaying family practices does not just relate to issues of judgement though. What is clear from this discussion is that families perform activities for a variety of reasons, and one of those may be to demonstrate to themselves, and others, that they are a 'family'. This is an important consideration when examining a component of family life, such as reading practices. When applying these ideas to the concept of reading, this shifts the focus from the question 'How do families do reading?' to 'What does reading do for families?' as now discussed.

What does reading do for families?

There has been a vast amount of research exploring reading and families, but it is fair to say that most of this has focused on the ways in which family reading practices support children's language development (Sawyer et al., 2016; Aikens & Barbarin, 2008; Senechal & LeFevre, 2002). In contrast, it is hard to find research that has sought to understand what reading does for the family, yet this is exactly what needs to be understood if we want to encourage and support shared reading practices in the home. The first step is to recognise that shared reading does take place in many homes, but it may not necessarily be regarded as a 'literacy' activity; for this reason it is important to conceptualise shared reading as a family practice that may take place for a wide variety of reasons.

When one regards reading with young children as a family practice, we can begin to see that it is not just a *literacy practice,* but the activity provides opportunities for families to achieve intimacy and connections with each other. For James (2013), everyday activities such as sharing family meals and watching television shows together facilitate a sense of 'connectedness', something that Smart (2007) argues is crucial to socialisation. Indeed, research suggests that while parents read with their children for many different reasons, they often report that being 'close' with their child, and wanting to have an enjoyable time, is a main aim of shared reading activity (Audet et al., 2008). Similarly, Alexander (2013: 180) also found that the parents in her study spoke of shared reading as a way of connecting physically and emotionally with their children, with Alexander reporting that:

All of the parents talked about the importance of bonding by 'snuggling,' 'cuddling,' 'being together,' or other such expressions of physical closeness. The parents were also seemingly concerned with the growth of the child's sense of security and trust, which is the foundation of his socio-personality and identity (Erikson, 1968) and critical to his cognitive development, as when they said that story time made the child feel 'loved,' 'special,' 'safe,' and 'watched over.'

Further research indicates that reading can also help to establish routines and structure within family life, which is seen as being especially beneficial when the family includes small children. Studies have suggested that establishing regular family routines encourage organisation within the family, cohesion and a sense of belonging (Fiese, 2002), given that there is a degree of emotional investment in carrying out routines, which can help to cement strong family relationships (Fiese & Everhart, 2008). However, families may also develop routines as a way of managing aspects of everyday life.

This is particularly evident in relation to the 'bedtime story' (discussed in further detail in the next chapter), which is often used as part of a bedtime routine for young children. The medical profession recommends that families promote a regular bedtime routine 'as a key factor in the promotion of not only healthy sleep, but also of broad development and wellbeing in early childhood' (Mindell & Williamson, 2017: 93). The characteristics of a bedtime routine often include a bath, oral hygiene and a bedtime story, which together sends a signal to the child that the day is over and it is time to go to sleep. This was also highlighted by Nichols (2000) in her study of middle-class Australian parents' involvement in young children's literacy. Nichols found that these parents generally had two main agendas for story reading at night; like Alexander (2013) found, one was to create space to bond with their child, but a second function was to help settle their child for the night. For many of the parents in Nichols' study, the evening routine was not necessarily easy, given that many competing demands were often placed on parents at this time of the day as they struggled to juggle meal preparation and household chores with settling young children down for the night. Nichols (2000: 320) reported that bedtime story reading therefore fulfilled another function, that of 'of balancing the distribution of parenting labour at a labour-intensive time of day', which enabled 'one parent to undertake evening domestic duties without the additional responsibility of childcare'.

What is interesting to note in Nichols' study, is that even though parents reported that the evening routine was often a time of 'heavy' demand, bedtime stories for their children quickly became 'a highly routinised practice', which was clearly prioritised in these homes. As discussed, reading at bedtime performed a number of functions including an opportunity to bond with the child and performed a role in settling children down to sleep for the night. However, Nichols' data also suggested that for many of these parents, and mothers in particular, there was a social expectation that they would read with their children. This is exemplified in Nichols' (2000: 317) observation:

In middle-class Australia, when a woman becomes a mother, she is expected to take up her literacy work. Advice available in magazines and books often assumes links between parenting and forms of literacy work.

This brings us back to the ways in which families come to display certain practices in order fulfil a social norm or expectation. Nichols is suggesting that society expects middle-class mothers to take a lead role in providing literacy education to their children, evidenced in the fact that a significant number of mothers in her sample said, without being asked, 'that they had read, or believed in reading to children from the youngest possible age' (318). Nichols' study demonstrates how the practice of reading to young children is not only seen to be 'good' for children but is regarded by society as a feature of 'good parenting'. This was repeatedly confirmed in Nichols' data; for example, one participant reported that she had been 'taught about early reading in the same instructional setting as she had been taught about birthing and infant care' (381). Moreover another participant, the only one to have reported that she did not read with her young child, stated her awareness of the fact that she was contravening popular belief when she said, 'I know people say you should read right from the word "go" to babies, but I don't think we ever did that much' (318).

This suggests that shared reading may offer parents the opportunity to display their parenting and demonstrate that they are doing the 'right thing' for their children. However, this can be highly challenging for individuals who, for various reasons, may struggle to read with their child. This issue was raised by Skinner (2013) who conducted research with mothers with dyslexia; interviews with these mothers revealed that they had a strong desire to read with their children in order to perform the role of 'good mother', but felt that their dyslexia hindered their ability to accomplish this due to their own difficulties with reading. All of Skinner's participants said that even though they generally enjoyed reading to their children, it was problematic, and they sometimes avoided reading for this reason. For example one participant reported, 'I love reading aloud to him but I hate it when I'm reading it wrong' while another said 'I always kind of made an excuse' (Skinner, 2013: 89–90).

Skinner's study reveals the tensions that can arise for parents who want to fulfil the requirement to execute their 'literacy work' (Nichols, 2000) but may be hindered from doing so. Yet there is surprisingly little research into this issue from the perspective of parents. As yet we know very little about the ways in which these social pressures may impact on parents within the context of their everyday family lives. What is more, while there is a great deal of research focusing on the benefits of shared reading for children (Baker, 1999; Bus et al., 1995; Sénéchal & Young, 2008), parents' and children's involvement in shared reading (Saracho, 2017; Martin-Chang & Gould, 2012) and factors influencing shared reading activity (Kucirkova et al., 2018; Lin et al., 2015), very little is known about what shared reading does for families. Yet, this is a critical starting point if we are to find ways of supporting families with shared reading activity in their homes. The research presented in this book was designed to do exactly that – to begin with families and understand how shared reading operates within families from various social and cultural backgrounds.

Conclusion

This chapter has shown how reading is a value-laden activity, embedded in discourses of power and authority and shaped by the various systems within which an individual resides. Moreover, reading is also a fluid construct, influenced by shifting textual landscapes and the needs of a changing society. For a child, this means that learning to read is a highly complex phenom-enon. In this chapter we have shown how definitions of what reading is, and what it means to be 'a reader', can be found in both the home and school contexts, meaning that young children come to understand the various ways in which reading is defined, used, valued and represented as they navigate their way through these domains on their paths to becoming readers.

Given the dominance of the school discourse, it is particularly important to understand how reading operates within families, yet very little is known about the ways in which reading is constructed, developed and practiced in homes and what the practice does for families. This is especially true of shared reading with young children, which has tended to be researched from the perspective of 'educational endeavour', rather than understanding what it is, how it functions within families and what families gain from the practice. Having examined reading from a sociological perspective in this chapter, the next chapter builds on this by looking specifically at shared reading, exploring the ways in which complex dynamics of class, culture and ethnicity can have an impact not only on shared reading activity, but on what it means for families.

3

SHARED READING PRACTICES

Having explored sociological perspectives as applied to reading in the previous chapter, we now turn to look specifically at what is known about shared reading practices and the factors that influence parent–child reading in the home. Beginning with an overview of what is meant by the term 'shared reading', we examine what is currently known about the reasons why parents do and do not read with their children. Recognising the limitations of this research, we then draw on the iconic studies of Heath (1982) and Brooker (2002), as well as more recent research, to show how shared reading activity connects with factors such as culture, ethnicity and social factors. In order to illustrate this, we focus attention on the 'bedtime story', showing how activities such as bedtime stories are deeply embedded in a socio-cultural discourse. Together this shows that shared reading is a highly complex phenomenon, influenced not only by social and cultural structures, but by the unique and specific features of everyday family life.

Defining 'shared reading'

As mentioned in the Introduction, it is surprisingly difficult to find a definition in the literature for the term 'shared reading'. Though the focus in this book is on shared reading with young children, it must be acknowledged that the term is used to describe the sharing of text in groups, many of which are made up of adults. This, for example, is particularly evident in the work of The Reader Organisation, who orchestrate shared reading groups within a wide variety of contexts such as criminal justice settings, care homes, community centres and hospitals. With an emphasis on reading aloud, The Reader Organisation define shared reading as:

> … a powerful group experience that sparks connection, reflection and discovery. By providing a creative and safe space to explore our inner lives and develop meaningful relationships with others, Shared Reading improves wellbeing and builds community.

While it is clearly the case that shared reading is an activity that can take place within groups of adults, this book is concerned with home shared reading practices with young children. We are therefore defining shared reading as an activity where a child is engaged in focusing on a text with another person (usually an adult) for a sustained period of time. During this time, the joint attention on a text will usually results in a shared construction of meaning.

As discussed in this book, and elsewhere, the fact that we now live in a 'digital age' (Merchant, 2007; Starkey, 2012) means that the texts used in shared reading may be digital or paper-based. Some argue that we are currently living in a period of transition from paper to screen, with Mangen and van der Weel (2016:117) stating that 'screens are replacing paper as the main reading substrate' and this is influencing reading in early years as well as primary and secondary education. While this may well be true in a variety of contexts, we take the view in this book that the texts on offer to parents and children for the purposes of shared reading are not transitioning from screen to paper but may simply include both. What is more, the research evidence suggests that there is little value in trying to distinguish between different types of media in the context of shared reading activity. We know that many young children are now reading on screen, for example, using apps on tablets (Merchant, 2015), and we also know that paper-based books are still regularly purchased by adults and read to their children (Egmont, 2013). In other words, we know that digital and paper texts are used within a shared reading context. Given that research that has attempted to understand the benefits of sharing screen texts in comparison with book texts has produced inconsistent and often conflicting results (Yuill & Martin, 2016; Ross et al., 2016), we are less concerned with understanding differences between digital and paper-based reading, but are focused on the aim to support families in using text, in whatever form it takes, within shared reading activity.

Having established in earlier chapters that shared reading involves joint and focused attention on a text, it is relevant to point out at this stage that the activity has been further categorised as 'reading to children' and 'listening to children read' (Martin-Chang & Gould, 2012), thus highlighting the directionality of the reading as being either adult-to-child or child-to-adult. While these activities are quite different from one another, research suggests that children gain different things from listening to a story in comparison with reading a text to an adult. For example, a number of studies report that adult-to-child reading does not, in itself, lead to a measurable increase in children's reading and writing skills (Aram & Biron, 2004; Aram & Levin, 2002; Frijters et al., 2000). This sits with the fact that research has shown that the amount of child-to-adult reading that takes place in the home is a stronger predictor of children's reading skill, than adult-to child reading (Hewison & Tizard, 1980; Tizard, Schofield & Hewison, 1982). What is more, as studies have also shown that both parents and teachers tend to focus on 'meaning-related rather than code-related (text) information' (Hindman et al.,

2008, p. 330), when reading to children, this suggests that adults give more attention to 'literacy acquisition training' (Martin-Chang & Gould, 2012: 855) when children read to them.

At first glance, this could appear to suggest that child-to-adult reading is more beneficial than adult-to child reading, however this far from the case. As already stated, adult-to-child reading is strongly associated with the development of children's oral language (Sénéchal & LeFevre, 2001; Bus et al., 1995). What is more Sénéchal and LeFevre (2002) demonstrated that children's exposure to books helped to develop vocabulary and listening comprehension skill, which in turn influenced their reading in the third grade. While this may well be the case, this also suggests that aims for shared reading are heavily embedded in a concern for the acquisition of literacy skill; however, as this book goes on to demonstrate, this is to radically underestimate the affordance of shared reading activity. Indeed, further studies have shown that reading to children is associated with a host of benefits including 'bonding' and 'enjoyment' (Audet et al., 2008) as well as promoting a love of reading (Weinberger, 1996).

Together this suggests that it is probably not helpful to spend much time distinguishing between adult-to-child reading and child-to-adult. Firstly, a focus on this distinction suggests that the activities are mutually exclusive, yet this is not necessarily the case; it is perfectly possible for adult-to-child and child-to adult reading to take place within the same activity. For example, even in their comparison of adult-to-child and child-to-adult reading sessions, Martin-Chang and Gould (2012) found that there was considerable overlap between the two; for example parents were reported to be less likely to focus on the printed text when they were reading to their children, in comparison with their children reading to them; however, they did still acknowledge the printed text, even though this tended to be given a secondary role during adult-to-child reading.

Secondly, while it is useful, for the purposes of definition, to consider the directionality of shared reading, much of the research indicates that the activity is somewhat adult-led and adult-directed. This seems to be the case whether the child is reading to the adult or not. Yet it would be a serious mistake to assume that shared reading is always initiated by adults or that young children are always at the mercy of the adults' management of the activity. As discussed in Chapter 6 later in this book, the research reported in this book found that much of the shared reading activity conducted in the home was in fact child-led. What is more, many of the parents reported that this was something that they valued and wanted to encourage. It is therefore really important to be aware from the outset, that shared reading is not something that is always done to children; as this book will go on to demonstrate, shared reading is often an activity in which even the youngest children are able to exert agency. They can, and do, have control over what is read, who reads with them, when and where they read and how the activity is structured.

Shared reading is therefore a literacy event, or indeed family practice, where a text is central in the joint production of meaning between people. But there is more to shared reading than the basic components of person and text; we must acknowledge the various ways in which the activity is 'relational' (Gergen, 2009). By this we mean recognising that social life can be more fully understood when we see the self as a point of intersection where many different relations meet. Therefore, as Papacharissi (2012) neatly articulates, we are evolving 'beyond individualism to understand societies as webs of relations rather than as assemblages of connected or disconnected individuals'. In this respect, understanding shared reading is about understanding the relationship between the readers and the goals and purposes they each have for the shared reading experience. It is also about the individual relationship each reader has with the text, for example understanding how each participant in the activity connects personally with the text being read. Moreover, each reader has their own relationship with 'reading', which will in turn influence the activity. This is discussed in detail in Chapter 8, which reports on the ways in which personal relationships with reading influenced the shared reading activity of the participants included in the study reported in this book. But before we examine these ideas in more detail it is useful to consider what is already known about the reasons why parents read with their children.

Why do parents read with their children?

Parents read with their children for many different reasons, yet research suggests that the phenomenon remains poorly understood. Over the years, researchers have invested considerable time in trying to understand why parents choose to read with their children. This stems from the argument that parental beliefs in relation to literacy influence children's literacy development (DeBaryshe, 1995; Sonnenschein et al., 1996); therefore underlining the importance of understanding what motivates parents to begin and maintain shared reading in the home. In 2008, Audet et al. conducted two related studies to investigate parents' goals for shared reading; the first surveyed 294 parents of early school-aged children, while the second study surveyed and observed a different sample of 119 parents. The studies revealed that parents had five distinct goals for shared book reading which were: to 'stimulate development'; to 'foster reading'; to 'bond with the child'; to 'soothe the child'; and to 'enjoy books'. However, the goals of 'enjoying reading' and 'bonding with their children' were rated most highly by parents with children at each grade.

The goal to enjoy reading together appears to be a priority for many parents, and there is evidence to suggest that having parents who prioritise enjoyment as a goal for reading is beneficial for children. For example Baker, Serpell and Sonnenschein (1995) found that children who come from homes which promote literacy as a source of entertainment are more likely to become intrinsically motivated to read. Similarly, Baker, Scher and Mackler (1997; 69) also found that parents who reportedly believed that reading is a source of entertainment 'have children with more positive views about reading than do parents who emphasize the skills aspect of reading development'.

What this shows is that parents value the role of enjoyment within shared reading activity, and this in turn is linked with children developing positive attitudes towards reading; however, this does raise questions about the factors that promote enjoyment. While the current literature only hints at this, one of the factors does seem to relate to the fact that many parents see shared reading as an opportunity to get close to their child and bond. For example, in their study of a reading programme for mothers and their babies, Harman and Jones (1999) found that these mothers not only organised more frequent family book reading sessions but focused on the emotional bond between themselves and their children. Similarly, in a more recent study of a Flemish reading programme for couples and their babies, Vanobbergen et al. (2009) found that parents greatly stressed the affective side of the reading activity, which resulted in their creating more reading rituals in their own homes.

It is therefore not surprising to find that proponents in attachment theory have shown a considerable interest in shared reading. It should be recognised that studies into attachment theory, many of which operate within a developmental paradigm, have tended to binarise the relationship between parent and young child into the categories of 'secure attachment' and 'insecure attachment'. Yet much further study, including the research reported in this book, would challenge this view, arguing that a child's development, including the development of their relationships, is particular to each individual and influenced by the unique socio-cultural environment of the child (Gauvain, 2005). For this reason we maintain that it is important to be cautious about the use of such definitive categorisations when seeking to understand the complexity of relationships; however, it is helpful to understand what these studies identified regarding the link between parent–child engagement and shared reading, in exploring what is currently known about parents' motivations for reading with their children.

For example, Bus et al. (1997) considered the relationship between parent–child attachment and the quantity and quality of book reading. High-quality book reading was characterised by efforts to encourage initiatives by the child, while low ratings were given to statements and actions reflecting inflexibility (for example, if the child turned the page and the adult went back because the page was not yet finished). Having compared toddlers and their parents who were described as being 'securely attached', with those described as being 'insecurely attached', Bus et al. (1997) concluded that high-quality book reading was associated with secure attachment. This link between parent–child attachment and book reading was also explored by Bingham (2007) who found that children who experience emotionally supportive, sensitive and interesting parent–child book reading at home may therefore be more likely to explore and read books on their own. Similarly, Bergin (2001) also found that early, fluent readers had more positive parent–child interaction during shared reading than late, non-fluent readers. Together this research is suggesting that strong emotional interaction between parent and child can lead to more positive outcomes for children in terms of their own reading. We feel this is important because it indicates that the parental reading goal of bonding is not only good for the relationship between child and parent but could also have a positive impact on the child's own relationship with reading as well as their developing skills in reading. However, we would also encourage caution around the claim that there is a causal link between 'secure' attachment and child reading skill. Concepts such as 'attachment', parent–child interaction and relationships with reading are highly complex and cannot be fully understood through an analysis of the kind of measures employed in these reported studies. This underlines a need for more qualitative research to explore and understand the factors that motivate parents to read with their children.

Research has identified that enjoying reading and bonding are important goals for parents in shared reading activity in the home; however, studies have also shown that parents are concerned about skill-orientated factors. Having explored views about early literacy instruction and the shared reading behaviours of 19 mothers and their 5- to 6-year-old children, DeBaryshe et al. (2000) concluded that most of the parents in this sample held 'eclectic views' on early literacy instruction. In other words, most of these mothers valued both 'code knowledge' (such as skills to decode print) and 'meaning' (making sense of the text) and reported that they used strategies to promote both sets of skills when reading with their children. DeBaryshe et al. found that while most parents tended to value decoding skills and an ability to make sense of print, children of the more 'code-orientated' mothers had the highest tested performance in areas such as story grammar and vocabulary, while children of the more 'meaning-orientated' mothers tended to have more mother–child reading and writing sessions and were more likely to write on their own. Interestingly, DeBaryshe et al. (2000: 130) came to the conclusion that children of both 'code-orientated' and 'meaning-orientated' mothers were advantaged; however, the overall disadvantage 'fell on children of mothers who endorsed neither code- nor meaning-based strategies' as 'their children showed the least developed literacy skills'. However, this research tells us very little about the ways in which parental goals for their children's skill-orientated reading development fit with other factors that may influence shared reading activity in the home.

Though limited, some research has examined parents' goals for shared reading activity that extend beyond enjoyment, bonding and reading skill acquisition. For example, Alexander (2013) found that parents also used shared reading as a means of strengthening their child's religious and cultural identity. Alexander set out to explore parental attitudes about reading bed-time stories with families who had participated in the programme PJ Library; PJ Library (the PJ stands for pyjamas!) sends out free Jewish children's books and music to Jewish and interfaith families on a monthly basis by subscrip-tion. Having interviewed four families, Alexander found that these parents used these stories to help their children identify themselves as a Jew and connect them with the Jewish community.

When we consider the question 'Why do parents read with their chil-dren?', we see that parents report a number of different goals for shared reading activity; however, the picture is far from clear. Firstly, the studies upon which this assertion is based have tended to isolate parental goals for shared reading, with little attempt being made to understand how these goals fit together. Yet this is not how family life works! Secondly, and in connection with this, these studies pay little regard to the role of the socio-cultural con-text in understanding why shared reading may happen. Each reader, whether a child or an adult, comes to the activity with beliefs and values that are influenced by the social and cultural context within which they are situated. Shared reading, like many other literacy events, is not a neutral practice. In order to illustrate this, we are now going to examine a particular shared reading event – the bedtime story. The reading of bedtime stories is a highly value-laden concept, influenced by factors such as the social, cultural and ethnic background of the family. In considering bedtime stories and reading routines, we now take a close look at the ways in which shared reading is influenced by socio-cultural discourses including those related to class, cul-ture and ethnicity.

Bedtime stories and reading routines

For some families, reading to young children as part of a bedtime routine is seen as being something that is simply expected. Nichols (2000: 319) pointed out, in her study of 56 middle-class parents of young children, that to connect reading with young children's bedtime is often so 'taken for granted' that this association can be seen as 'natural'. What is more, reading bedtime stories can often be viewed as part of 'good parenting', sitting alongside other socially desirable family routines such as eating together and ensuring that children brush their teeth regularly. But accepting the view that reading to children before bedtime is a natural part of family routine, and indeed presents a mark of 'good parenting', is deeply problematic.

The reason for this was probably first evidenced in the ground-breaking work of Heath (1982) who conducted ethnographic research into the literacy practices of three communities in the south-eastern United States (Piedmont Carolinas). Heath's study drew attention to the role of children's social and cultural context with regard to shared reading in homes. This study vividly demonstrates that activities such as the bedtime story are not 'natural' home practices for all children; the bedtime story as a construct is deeply embedded in a specific socio-cultural discourse, meaning that it cannot be taken for granted that it is a universal practice. What is more, Heath's study also showed, with alarming clarity, that children who engage in shared reading activities, such as bedtime stories, were more likely to be developing knowledge and skills that aligned with school, thus offering preparation for, and enabling 'success' at school to begin from the outset.

Before we describe Heath's work, which has been undoubtedly pivotal in literacy studies, it is necessary to say a few words about the language Heath employed in describing the different communities in the study. The communities that Heath studied were named and defined by Heath (1982: 49) as *Maintown* – a 'mainstream middle-class school-orientated culture', *Roadville* – 'a white mill community of Appalachian origin' and *Trackton* – 'a black mill community of recent rural origin'. Reading Heath's work today, the description of a middle-class community as 'mainstream', and a working-class community as 'non-mainstream', suggests a normalisation of the middle classes, and an 'othering' of the working classes. While it must be remembered that Heath's work is almost 40 years old, and we have since learned much about the importance of avoiding labels in research that may imply judgements or prejudice, we do need to recognise that cycles of disadvantage can be perpetuated by the use of such terminology. Such labels position those who are not white middle class as something 'other' to the norm. Though Heath's work must be challenged on these grounds, her study was in fact one of the first to illuminate the consequences of this very issue, in relation to the perceived normativity of the school discourse.

In brief, what Heath reported was that far from literacy practices being 'natural', children 'take' from the culture within which they live and learn the literate traditions of their own environment. What is more, being exposed to the repetition of certain literacy events sets patterns of behaviour that can have particular advantages for children, with Heath arguing that the bedtime story is one such 'major literacy event'. She wrote:

> In both popular and scholarly literature, the 'bedtime story' is widely accepted as a given – a natural way for parents to interact with their child at bedtime. Commercial publishing houses, television advertising, and children's magazines make much of this familiar ritual, and many of their sales pitches are based on the assumption that in spite of the intrusion of television into many patterns of interaction between parents and children, this ritual remains. Few parents are fully conscious of what bedtime story-reading means as preparation for the kinds of learning and displays of knowledge expected in school.
>
> (Heath, 1982, 51)

What Heath found was that children growing up in the community she called 'Maintown' were not only getting bedtime stories (among other literacy events) but were being encouraged to engage with texts in a way that ran parallel with the expectations of school. By the time these children had entered school they were, for example, skilled at giving information, they knew how to perform in their interactions with text and they had learned how to listen and wait for cues which signalled that it was time 'to show off' the knowledge they had acquired from their engagement with texts. In Heath's detailed analysis of literacy interaction in homes, she demonstrates how children within this community had learned how to not only 'take meaning' from text, but also talk about it in ways that are valued in the school context.

This differed substantially from 'Roadville' and 'Trackton', which Heath reported were both communities that valued success in school and urged their children to do well; however, she claimed that children from both these communities were considered to be unsuccessful in school, according to the expectations of the school discourse. The children in the 'Roadville' cohort were read to in their pre-school years, and their home literacy practices prepared them well for the first few years of formal schooling. For example, these children entered school with knowledge that was valued in school, such as knowing portions of the alphabet, numbers, colours and so on. As parents had used questions in the home that encouraged the children to give explanations, they consequently knew how to answer these kinds of questions in school, which again contributed towards initial success in school. However, the children were not used to literacy interactions, which, for example, asked them to give their opinion, or encouraged them to apply knowledge from one context (e.g. a book) to another (e.g. real life). Heath reported that as a result, 'Roadville' children did not maintain this early 'success', and achievement tended to drop once they entered the third or fourth grades, given that their attainment was measured against criteria governed by the school discourse.

The home literacy experiences of children in Trackton were different again. This was evident in a number of ways, but one clear difference was that Heath's observations indicated that children in Trackton were rarely read to. Heath reported that bedtime stories were not common practice, partly because they did not have the bedtime routines that were visible in other communities. Heath reported:

> Since children are usually left to sleep whenever and wherever they fall asleep, there is no bedtime or naptime as such. At night, they are put to bed when adults go to bed or whenever the person holding them gets tired. Thus, going to bed is not framed in any special routine. Sometimes in a play activity during the day, an older sibling will read to a younger child, but the latter soon loses interest and squirms away to play. Older children often try to 'play school' with younger children, reading to them from books and trying to ask

questions about what they have read. Adults look on these efforts with amusement and do not try to convince the small child to sit still and listen.

(Heath, 1982, 65)

In reading Heath's account, it is important to remember that her observations of the literacy practices in homes were situated within a discourse that privileged white, middle-class constructions of schooling. Keeping this in mind, we notice that Heath sees fit to report that the adults mentioned in the quote above do not try to 'convince' the smaller children 'to sit and listen' when they are playing school with their older siblings. Sitting and listening is clearly a 'schooled' expectation that Heath is very well aware of, and she is stating that part of the reason why Trackton children may have struggled to succeed in the school system originated in the fact that they were not being 'trained' to follow the requirements of the school discourse from their earliest years. We must be clear that Heath was not suggesting that these parents should have been giving their children this formative experience; on the contrary Heath was pointing out that the schooling system was poorly prepared to support children whose home literacy experience did not match its own discourse.

This of course raises deep and serious questions about the ways in which, and the reasons why, some children may be disadvantaged within the school system. Given that this has substantial implications for the ways in which schools make judgements about children's attainment to this very day, it is important to be reminded of Heath's research. It is beyond the scope of this chapter to discuss Heath's account of the differences between the three communities in any further detail, but what is important to stress is that the children from all three communities responded differently to books in school, because they had each learned different methods and different ways of taking from books within the home. However, as the school system privileged the literacy skills that were reflected in the '*Maintown*' community only, this disadvantaged the children from '*Roadville*' and '*Trackton*' from the beginning of their schooling. This raises huge concerns about the ways in which schools promote beliefs about what counts as literacy and what literacy skills are valued in society; given that the acquisition of literacy skill is influenced by social and cultural contexts, this has major implications for many children entering the formal education system to this day.

In the years that followed Heath's pivotal study, many other researchers also found that factors such as class and culture can influence children's access to schooled literacy. This was highly apparent in the work of Brooker (2002) whose study of 16 four-year-old children, all from working-class backgrounds, revealed that ethnicity and culture can have a major impact on whether children succeed in school during their earliest years. Half of the children in Brooker's study were born and educated in the UK. For this group, their home language was English and their home culture was what Brooker described as 'English working class', though it should be noted that Brooker also pointed out that three of these children were of dual English and Afro-Caribbean heritage (2). The remaining eight children were from homes that Brooker described as 'Bangladeshi'; Brooker reported that all of the parents of these children were born in the province of Sylhet, and their home and work lives 'were almost entirely within the Bangladeshi community in the neighbourhood' (2). Six of the children were born in the UK, but two were born in Bangladesh and had moved to the UK when they were two years old.

Like Heath, Brooker also found that culture and community were critical factors in the extent to which children were prepared for their lives in school, given that the school discourse was dominated by a particular set of cultural expectations. What is particularly noteworthy about Brooker's study is that all the children were defined as 'disadvantaged', in that all came from working-class communities and none had the advantages of a middle-class upbringing; however, Brooker found that the children she described as 'English working class' had an easier transition into school than the children of Bangladeshi origin, because their home cultures fitted more closely with the expectations of schools. This was evidenced in numerous ways. For example, the children whose parents were born and educated in the UK were more likely to have experienced 'school-like' pre-school learning, in comparison with the children of Bangladeshi origin; this was apparent in the toys they were given, the activities they were involved in and the ways in which their parents interacted with them. For some of the children of Bangladeshi origin, home culture was so different from school that, as Brooker reported, they had to 'unlearn their home concept in order to acquire the learning behaviours approved in school' (151).

It is perhaps not surprising that one of Brooker's findings related specifically to bedtimes. Brooker observed that 'some' of the children whose parents were born in the UK, but 'none' of the children of Bangladeshi origin, received a 'nightly bedtime story routine' (57). While it is important to recognise that the reasons for this were to some extent individual, Brooker suggested that they were also shaped by the family's cultural background. To illustrate, Brooker's analysis revealed that the mothers born in the UK all shared a belief that 'children require firm and regular routines from earliest infancy' (48). This included establishing regular sleep routines, which meant that infants were 'put down to sleep' for naps at regular times during the day, and bedtimes were also governed by a regular routine. In contrast, the families of Bangladeshi origin tended to include their children in family life at all hours and thus did not expect their children to go to bed at a certain time in the evenings. When the children rose early to go to school, they would often nap after school, then join the family for an evening meal. What is more, some of these families did not compartmentalise their homes into 'bedrooms' and 'living spaces', as the UK-born parents did but, as Brooker (2002, 49) reports, they 'use their living space flexibly for eating and sleeping, juxtaposing their children's bikes and their babies' cots with large-scale food preparation'.

Given that bedtime stories fit into bedtime routines, with research showing that pre-schoolers who have regular bedtimes tend to have family members who spend time reading to them (Mindell et al., 2009), Brooker's analysis shows that it is naïve and misguided to assume that parents 'should' be reading bedtime stories to their children, because this would be to assume that all families instil the same routines into their children's daily lives. For the families of Bangladeshi origin in Brooker's study, children's integration into family life meant that bedtimes were not governed by routines, meaning that it was highly unlikely that bedtime stories would ever feature as part of everyday family life. The purpose of this discussion is not to make any judgement about the value of such routines for young children, but to demonstrate that activities such as bedtime stories may or may not fit within the everyday practices of families from different cultural backgrounds.

In looking back at the work of Heath and Brooker we are reminded that activities such as bedtime stories may be regarded as 'natural' within a dominant discourse, but of course this is simply not the case. These studies remind us that home literacy practices may be influenced by factors such as socio-cultural context; however, it would be a mistake to suggest that the inclusion of activities such as bedtime stories into family routines are always socially and culturally determined. As Brooker herself points out, while we must acknowledge the role of culture on family routines, 'children's home culture is a complex combination of family circumstances past and present' (57). In other words, we need to look beyond the broad positionings of socio-cultural context to understand why parents may or may not read bedtime stories to their children.

This was highlighted recently in a study by Kelly et al. (2016) who examined the bedtime routines of 20 low- and middle-income African American families and their pre-schoolers. Aware that many quantitative studies have tended to either omit the experiences of African American families, or compare them with white middle-class families with the conclusion that their family bedtimes routines are in some ways 'deficient' (Hale et al., 2009; Hale et al., 2011; Milan et al., 2007), Kelly et al. conducted interviews with African American caregivers from diverse socio-economic backgrounds, to understand the bedtime experiences African American pre-schoolers have with literacy.

Kelly et al.'s study showed that parents within both socio-economic groups did read bedtime stories to their children, though this was more prevalent among the middle-income families, yet even within socio-economic groups, individual factors influenced shared reading practices in the home. Family support seemed to be a particularly important factor influencing bedtime reading as illustrated below:

> Low-income caregivers who were home full-time and had residential spouses, reported consistent engagement in shared reading. However, low-income mothers who were single and had the lowest levels of income did not include shared reading in their discussion of children's bedtime routines at all. This suggests that there were within-group differences in shared reading at bedtime among low-income families that may be connected to the availability of additional financial resources and social support.
>
> (Kelly et al., 2016: 188)

What this research shows is that the complexity of family life can impact on bedtime shared reading, especially when there is a lack of financial and social support. Given that the middle-class Australian parents in Nichols' (2000) study reported that the early evening was a particularly challenging time of day, with one mother referring to it as the 'arsenic hour', and that reading bedtime stories tended to be shared between mothers and fathers, it is no great surprise that Kelly et al. found that the parents in their study who were least likely to report that they read with their children at bedtimes were low-income single mothers. This strongly suggests that factors such as support in the home and financial stability may influence shared reading activity, particularly as part of a bedtime routine.

By drawing on various studies conducted over the last four decades, we can clearly see that the 'bedtime story' is not in any way a natural phenomenon, but that these practices are deeply embedded in a socio-cultural discourse and are influenced by factors such as culture, class and ethnicity as well as access to financial and social support. Importantly, the research discussed above has also shown that engagement in activities such as bedtime stories can serve to advantage children as they start school, as these activities correspond with the expectations of the school discourse. What this also goes to show is that shared reading is complex, and that in order to understand such practices, we need to understand specific features of family life. We need to take time to understand how individual parents navigate shared reading practices with the everydayness of family life and the extent to which it does and does not fit with their own circumstances, culture, beliefs and goals. This was exactly the aim of the research reported in this book. Before this is presented though, it is useful to look at the research to date that has attempted to understand why parents may not read with their children. For clarity, this is not to cast judgement on parents in any way, but rather to understand some of the factors that have already been identified in published research.

Barriers to shared reading

Given that there is such a substantial body of literature reporting the benefits of shared reading in the home, there is surprisingly little research into the factors that may prevent parents from reading with their children, or cause barriers to shared reading activity. From the studies that have attempted to understand this, barriers have been identified which fall into the three main categories of being 'parent-centred', 'child-centred' and 'structural' (e.g. access to books) (Lin et al., 2015).

In their cross-sectional analysis of variables associated with parents' reading to young children, Harris et al. (2007) identified parent-centred barriers, such as parents being too busy and working, as factors that prevented them from reading with their children; however, it should be noted that these barriers received relatively low ratings compared with structural barriers. In a further study that explored that contextual factors and infant characteristics predicting whether parents read aloud to their 8-month-old infants, Karrass et al. (2003: 134) found that parenting stress and 'general hassles' were a barrier to shared reading in the home. Studies that have identified child-centred barriers have reported that parents find it hard to read to a child that seems disinterested in the activity or frustrated (Bergin, 2001); however, the literature is very unclear about the extent to which these factors, in isolation from other factors, actually prevent parents from reading with their children. The structural barriers reported in the literature included factors such as distraction in the home and a lack of access to reading materials, with Harris et al. (2007: 264) reporting that the participants in their study 'indicated that the cost of books was their greatest barrier to reading to their children'.

It would be easy to assume that findings such as this provide 'the answer' to supporting families with shared reading in the home. For example, given that the cost of books has been identified as a barrier to shared reading, then it would stand to reason that the provision of books, especially to families on a low income, would encourage parents to read with their children. Indeed, there are a number of organisations that offer books to families with young children, with Booktrust and Dolly Parton's Imagination Library being major book-gifting organisations known for their work across the world. There is no doubt that these organisations provide a crucial role in encouraging reading in homes, but it would be a mistake to conclude that the mere provision of books will ensure that all families read with their children.

To return to Harris et al.'s (2007) study, they found that access to books was a major issue for many of the participants in their study, as mentioned above; however, they also found that despite the relative lack of books in many homes, very few parents reported that they used their local library. In addition to this, a sizeable proportion of the parents also reported 'a lot' of difficulty in selecting good books for their children, though self-efficacy in reading did not seem to be an issue within this sample. Harris et al. (2007: 266) therefore concluded:

> Thus, if mothers or significant others believed that reading may be beneficial to their children, if books were available at home, and if parents perceived fewer barriers, they were more likely to read books with their children regardless of their self-efficacy to select books and their education level. Although self-efficacy to select books was not a significant predictor, it was related to having more books in the home, a perception of fewer barriers and greater perception of benefits to reading.

This shows that the reasons why parents may not read with their children are not only tied to practical issues, such as access to books, but are influenced by their perceptions of barriers to reading and their perceptions of the benefits of reading. The concept of self-efficacy seems to be especially significant as Harris et al. are here reporting that self-efficacy in selecting books was connected to having more books in the home, perceiving fewer barriers to reading and having stronger perceptions of the benefits of reading to children. Building on these findings, Lin et al. (2015; 3) also found that mothers with a higher self-efficacy in reading perceived fewer barriers; however, they argued that self-efficacy in reading could even help these mothers to 'buffer against' other perceived barriers.

While these studies go some way in helping us to understand barriers to shared reading in families, this also underlines how complex and multifaceted the issue is. This chapter has highlighted a number of factors that may both motivate and discourage parents from reading with their children; however, it has also shown how shared reading is deeply embedded within social and cultural discourses. This means that shared reading activity, as some may see it, may simply not 'fit' within the context of everyday life for particular families.

Conclusion

We know that shared reading is highly beneficial for young children, yet we also know that not all parents read with their children. It is therefore important to understand the factors that not only encourage parents to read with their children, but the barriers that may inhibit, discourage or prevent shared reading from taking place in homes. As this chapter has shown, studies such as those by Harris et al. (2007) and Lin et al. (2015) have been helpful in identifying specific barriers to shared reading; however, in both these studies the research design restricted parents to selecting barriers from a list of preexisting factors rather than providing opportunities for parents to discuss how shared reading features in their everyday lives. This is important given that much of our current understanding about the ways in which shared reading is influenced by socio-cultural discourses has come from qualitative research that has taken time to understand how families work (Heath, 1982; Brooker 2002).

Our research was designed to enable parents to talk in detail about their lives with their young children and discuss the motivators and barriers to shared reading within the context of everyday family life. This study meets a clear need to understand how families considered to be living in areas of relative disadvantage, and from various cultural communities, perceive shared reading and implement it, as well as understand the factors that may influence such practices. The next chapter describes the research at the heart of this book and explains how the study was designed and how the data were collected and analysed.

4

RESEARCHING FAMILY LIVES

Introduction

Having recognised a need for interdisciplinary, qualitative study to research shared reading in families, this chapter introduces our study that was designed to explore shared reading in 29 families and explains the methods that were used to conduct this research. While academic convention often suggests a linear representation of research design and conduct, the reality is that qualitative research is a messy process, with unchartered territories to be encountered and navigated. Moreover, research that focuses on those aspects of our lives that take place behind closed doors adds to the complexity of this endeavour (Mauthner et al., 2002). As Chapters 2 and 3 have shown, reading is not a neutral activity; it is value laden, shaped by discourses of power and authority, yet it is embedded in the fabric of everyday life and relationships. We were therefore aware from the outset that we had to design a study that allowed participants to talk openly and comfortably about reading, given our recognition of the fact that reading is not detached from value and judgement in the wider world.

As discussed in the previous chapters, research into shared reading in homes has tended to focus on the ways in which family reading practices support children's language development (Sawyer et al., 2016; Aikens & Barbarin, 2008; Senechal & LeFevre, 2002). Very little research has attempted to understand the factors that motivate or inhibit shared reading activity, and where an attempt has been made, studies have tended to be quantitative in design, asking parents to select responses from pre-defined categories (see e.g. Lin et al., 2015). However, as already stated, if we are to understand shared reading practices in families, we recognised that we had to design research that sought to understand *families*, and their everyday family practices.

This was very much the starting point for this study. We then set about designing a study that would allow us to gain an insight into the routines, practices and relationships within families, with a view to understanding how shared reading did or did not fit within families' everyday lives. This focus meant that the study was not designed to establish generalisations as such, but rather to gain a depth of understanding that may be transferable to others. It was therefore clear from the outset that interviews would be an ideal research tool to use, as they would allow an opportunity for us to talk to our research participants in detail. However, the structure and content of these interviews demanded careful thought.

This chapter begins with an overview of research with families, recognising some of the complexities that are embedded in the process of researching families. Given this recognition, the chapter then presents an outline of the design of the research which is central to this book. Having justified a need to employ narrative techniques, we explain how we designed interviews to capture the essence of participants' everyday lives, and explore the ways in which shared reading did or did not fit within this. We then introduce the research participants and discuss some of the ethical issues arising from this study, especially in relation to conducting research in participants' homes. In connection with this, we also explore the complex issue of researcher positionality and the relationship between participant and researcher. The chapter is concluded with an outline of the process used to analyse the data, before concluding with some final reflections.

Researching families

Previous research into families and their lives has drawn upon a variety of different theories and theoretical frameworks. Similarly, this study was informed by work from within a number of different disciplines, including theories of literacy and family literacy practices, theories of socialisation and family practice and display. This was critical, as it meant that we were conceptualising shared reading as one of the many family practices that could be taking place in homes, rather than researching whether a specific literacy practice (shared reading) was taking place or not. This was a subtle but important step. As we have already seen, reading is not value-free – it is surrounded by constructs of judgement and is attached to issues of identity and worth. Therefore, we knew that if we really wanted to understand shared reading practices within a socially and culturally mixed sample, we had to design a study that allowed participants to talk freely about their lives, their families and their everyday activities. While participants were made aware of our interest in shared reading, we knew that reading activity, and shared reading in particular, had to be explored within the context of everyday family practices in order to encourage the production of meaningful data within a study that was also ethically sound. How this was achieved is discussed in detail a little later in this chapter.

Given the discussion about family practice and display presented in Chapter 2, we were aware that a first step in our research design was to recognise that the construct of 'family' is complex. We have already shown that there is little value in trying to define what 'a family' is, especially given that some have argued that, historically at least, the term 'family' has tended to evoke a notion of 'the white, middle class, heterosexual family' (Smart 2007: 30). Rather, we adopted Morgan's (2011) conceptualisation of the family as a unit that is defined by what they 'do' rather than who they 'are'. This brought us to Gabb's (2008) work, who asserts that these theorisations can be encapsulated as the 'post familial family', which acknowledges that relationships are not merely dictated by structure, but increasingly take into account the self-fulfilment of kinship, which moves beyond the boundaries of duty and obligation.

This further suggests that the term 'family' is also a fluid construct; as Morgan (2011) points out, factors such as cohabitation, divorce and single parenthood, as well as trends in perceptions of who constitutes family, may mean that membership changes over time. As a result we were led by our participants as to who constituted their family, and the analysis was informed by this notion that 'family' can mean different things to different people. We were aware that 'being family' may point towards kinship, residence or some other connection. For example, a parent may be biologically or legally related to a child but not reside with them, or conversely, an individual may occupy a parenting role, residing with a child and yet not be biologically or legally connected (Smart, 2007). What is more we were aware that constructs of 'family' can change over time, which again underlined a need for the participants to take the lead in defining who belonged to their own family.

Emphasising the notion of what families do, rather than who they are, sat very comfortably with our aim to focus on family practices. Drawing on the words of Phoenix and Brannen (2014: 12), we recognised that families offer 'an opportunity and context for understanding everyday habitual practices within wider social structures and at the intersection of time and space as they produce and reproduce identities'. In other words, we were aware that a carefully designed interview, which allowed us to understand shared reading as part of the everyday fabric of family practices, was not only methodologically appropriate but would help us to understand a phenomenon that is currently poorly understood.

However, research of this nature, which aims to understand not only a family practice, but the 'story' behind the practice, demands a particular kind of research design. This can be seen in a number of research studies including Pahl and Rowsell's (2010) work with children, adolescents and university students, which showed how objects can hold important meanings for individuals, families and communities, and can be linked to a sense of identity. By focusing on artefacts that were meaningful to the participants, Pahl and Rowsell conducted an in-depth study which demonstrated that objects are often significant 'because of the relationships or events with which they are associated' (Walsh, 2011: 501). Pahl and Rowsell's study shows that 'understanding families' is a complex endeavour but it can be achieved.

While it was clear that interviews would allow us, in this present study, to talk to families about their experiences and beliefs about shared reading, we were aware that these interviews would have to be very carefully constructed so as to ensure that data pertaining to the wider context of these activities was allowed to emerge.

In our quest to understand the wider context within which shared reading was embedded, we also drew on the work of Cole (1996), a cultural psychologist who focused on the link between culture and thought processes. In particular, his work examined the concept of *prolepsis*, where he argued that caregivers (usually mothers) look back into their own past in order to consider their children's futures. This sat firmly with our concern to understand the wider socio-cultural context of family reading, as it suggests that concerns for a child's education may be deeply embedded in the cultural and historical background of the parent. This was an important consideration for our study, as we realised that we needed to not only talk to parents about the reading practices that they shared with their children, but explore the parents' own relationship with reading, including any shared reading activity they may have been involved in when they were children.

Together this drove the decision to employ a narrative approach within the design of this study. Narrative approaches are well practiced in the fields of social and educational research, resulting in what has become known as the 'narrative turn' (Goodson et al., 2016). Given that narrative approaches are useful for exploring that which might be taken for granted (Phoenix & Brannen, 2013), this further supported our decision. There is a substantial body of literature that demonstrates how narrative inquiry has the potential to facilitate accounts of generation, culture, the life course, identity and everyday practices (Gabb, 2008), through the stories people tell. This might include the presentation of 'grand narratives' or 'big' stories, as seen in Thomas and Znacecki's (1918) stories on Polish peasants, or they might include profound personal experiences, as demonstrated in Ken Plummer's (2002) work *Telling Sexual Stories*, which is about individual's experience of 'coming out' sexually. However a narrative approach can also bring to light the smaller, everyday occurrences, which might at first appear mundane; for example, narrative studies have reported on events such as washing dishes (Martens, 2012) and showering (Shove, 2012).

As discussed in Chapter 2, shared reading can be perceived as an everyday family practice, to the point that it may even be 'taken for granted' by some. We were aware that important factors may have been deeply embedded in the minutia of everyday life, or 'hidden' within the social, cultural and historical background of individuals. It was therefore our job to make sure that we designed a study that allowed participants to talk about these details, because, as Jamieson et al. (2011:5) point out, 'aspects of families' lives may be hidden simply because of their apparent mundaneness to those involved .... indeed shared traditions and practices may be so taken for granted that they are unremarkable to participants themselves'. Given that, as Riessman (1993: 2–3) suggests, 'narratives of personal experience ... are ubiquitous in everyday life' and that 'telling stories about past events seems to be a universal human activity', we were confident that a narrative approach would allow us the best opportunity to not only access this data, but 'authorize the stories' (Fraser, 2004: 181), that would lead to new understandings about these practices.

Designing the study

This study is part of a broader programme of research titled 'Promoting Language Development by Shared Reading', funded by the Economic and Social Research Council (ESRC), led by the University of Liverpool from 2015 to 2018. The project as a whole sought to explore the impact of shared reading on children's language development including the identification of language boosting behaviours used by parents in shared reading and an exploration of how these behaviours impact children's language development. Some of these studies took the form of a reading intervention. Findings from these studies can be found in www.lucid.ac.uk/news-events-blog/blogs/it-is-not-easy-nor-simple-nor-cheap-to-improve-children-s-early-language-skills/. While the study reported in this book benefitted from being part of this larger project, it was a discrete study in its own right, collecting qualitative data in order to answer specific questions about the motivators and barriers to shared reading activity in homes.

Twenty-nine families were recruited to take part in this study; participants were recruited from two different cities in the north of England – we have called these cities Dalton and Barnwell. While both cities experienced decline in their local industries in the 1970s and 1980s, these cities have also experienced a degree of regeneration in recent decades. That said, both cities have high levels of deprivation, with Barnwell ranking more highly than Dalton in the Index of Multiple Deprivation. It should be noted that no attempt was made to draw any comparisons between participants from the two cities; the decision to recruit from two cities was simply to secure a wider sample base.

Participants in Dalton were recruited through a variety of strategies, including the distribution of a flyer to parents of nursery children at five schools. Additionally, face-to-face recruitment took place in playgroups, health visitor drop-in sessions and children's centres, in both low and mixed-income areas. A member of the research team attended these sessions and, with the permission of the setting, spoke to potential participants about the research. Only participants who had a child who had not yet started school were recruited. The participants' children were all aged 3 and 4 years, with the exception of three children who were 35 months, 31 months and 21 months.

Participants in Barnwell were all attending reading sessions as part of the wider project, as discussed above. These parents had already volunteered to be involved in the broader research project, which involved question-naire completion and an agreement to be filmed reading with their child. Parents were given information about the wider study and were asked if they would be interested in being interviewed about reading in their homes for a separate study (and the study that is the focus of this book). Potential participants provided their contact details and gave permission for a member of our research team to contact them. A week later, they were contacted by a researcher to discuss participation in the project. Although we initially made phone calls, we found text messages to be the most convenient means of doing this and were largely preferred by the participants. The participants' children were all aged 3–4 years.

Given that the participants in Barnwell were recruited through a different path from those in Dalton, and were already involved in an intervention study, this naturally had an impact on the research. All participants were made aware that our interest was in understanding shared reading practices, however as discussed in detail above, we felt it was imperative that we design interviews that allowed parents to talk firstly about their everyday lives, and then discuss the ways in which shared reading did, or did not fit within this. In reality, we found that this was more difficult to achieve with participants from Barnwell than Dalton. Because these participants were already involved in a reading intervention, they were more focused on reading than participants in Dalton; for example, these participants were more likely to talk about reading at an early point in the interview than those from Dalton. However, this was something that we had pre-empted, so we made sure that we spoke to participants from Barnwell specifically about the aims of the research and emphasised our concern to understand their everyday routines, activities and family practices.

The interviews

Given the need to allow participants to talk freely about their own lives, and present their own personal stories, interviews had to be semi-structured. This ensured that salient questions were asked and particular topics were discussed; however, we were also keen to encourage these parents to elaborate on their own responses and, in particular, talk in detail about their own experiences, beliefs and hopes. We began all interviews with questions that invited parents to talk about their children and their family routines including any activ-ities they engaged in regularly with their children. Although this research focused on a target child (most of whom were aged 3–4 years), parents were encouraged to talk about other siblings and the relationship between their children as well as other family members. If reading was mentioned during the course of the conversation, then we asked parents to elaborate on these activities. If reading was not mentioned, then we began to embed specific questions about reading activity into the interview. However, as mentioned above, given that we were also interested in exploring the ways in which parents' own relationships with reading may have influenced their shared reading practices with their children, we also asked questions about their memories of reading as a child, any shared reading they may have engaged with when they were children, and their reading practices as an adult.

These interviews led to an unfolding of the ways in which reading, and shared reading in particular, was contextualised within the minutiae of everyday family life and routines. This approach allowed an insight into many experiences and beliefs including parents' relationships with reading, their reading at school, their memories of reading with their own parents, their journey to becoming parents, their beliefs and practices regarding reading with their children and the various ways in which reading is cemented in the everyday context of family life. In other words, this approach generated 'thick' or 'rich' descriptions (Denzin, 1989; Plummer, 2001) that, when analysed, allowed an insight into the complexity of shared reading in families.

All interviews were conducted in participants' homes and were arranged at a time chosen by the participant. It was not necessary for this study for the children to be present during the interview; however, in many cases the children were with their parents while they were being interviewed. Conducting research in participants' own homes is clearly a privilege; however, this does raise a number of ethical issues, which will be discussed a little later in this chapter.

The participants

Although efforts were made to recruit fathers as well as mothers, the final sample consisted of twenty-eight mothers and one father. This was not surprising as most of the participants were recruited through attendance at pre-school activities, and it is well known that mothers still tend to be the main carers of pre-school age children (Fine, 2010), especially within certain communities. However, given the nature of the interviews, and the focus on 'the family', participants were encouraged to talk about all central characters in their children's lives, including mothers, fathers, siblings, grandparents, step-families and so on. This strategy proved to be very successful and the mothers in the study generally spoke at length about the fathers' involvement in family life and shared reading activity.

Participants were aged 21 to 36+ years, with the majority being in the 26–35 category. Of the 29 families participating in the study, 14 had two children and their children were predominantly aged between 3 and 5 years. We asked participants to select their ethnicity and these were categorised as follows: White British/Irish ($n=14$); Asian/Asian British ($n=7$), Mixed White and Other ($n=4$), Arab ($n=3$) and black (1). In relation to educational qualifications, 12 participants were educated to degree level or higher, 8 to General Certificate of Education (GCSE) level while 5 stated that they did not possess any formal qualifications. All participants lived in inner-city areas that were considered as relatively disadvantaged on the Indices of Multiple Deprivation. Table 4.1 provides an overview of the sample. In order to protect the identity of all participants, pseudonyms were given to all adults and children and have been used throughout this book.

Our position and ethical implications

While all research is bound by ethical implications, research that takes place in participants' homes carries a particular responsibility. This responsibility is first and foremost to the participants themselves, given that we are in the privileged position of being present in the private sphere of their home. This raises a number of issues for consideration such as ensuring that the participant is comfortable having a stranger (or relative stranger) in their home. The second responsibility is to the validity of the data itself; while this issue is not confined to research of this nature, if there is a power imbalance between participant and researcher, resulting in the participant feeling a need to provide responses that the researcher wants to hear rather than giving their own opinion, then this could pose a threat to the validity of the data. These two issues are tightly connected. This meant that we had to give very careful consideration to the relationship between participant and researcher in this study. On many levels we, as members of the research team, could be described as 'outsiders' to the participants; however, there were also factors that could help identify us an 'insiders'.

The insider/outsider dilemma is an important consideration and has been addressed in other studies. For example, Gregory and Ruby (2011) presented a detailed account of the ways in which being an outsider to their research community (Gregory) and an insider (Ruby) raised different issues with regard to researcher positionality. Given that this research explored the family literacy histories of Bangladeshi British families in East London, Gregory speaks of the fact that she recognised that as an English speaker of white Anglo background, she would not be able to be an 'insider' when visiting these families. Even though Gregory was experienced in conducting research in these communities, and was accompanied by a Bangladeshi British researcher who acted as a mediator, she reported 'I had still not quite anticipated the scope of my difficulties and the serious nature of the "faux pas" I would make as an "outsider"' (166). The examples that Gregory provides in this paper show that even experienced ethnographers can make assumptions about families that they may come to define as being culturally naïve. However, Gregory is also making the point that it is important to recognise for the outset if you are an 'outsider', rather than attempt to cross a boundary that is not possible.

Table 4.1 Table of participants

Name	Cohort	Age	Qualifications	Ethnicity	Child's name	Child age	Is this first child?	Number of children	Household composition	Household income bracket
1 Hadra	A	31–35	No formal qualifications	Asian British	Saira	3	No	2	Lives with the children's father	£24,000–£41,999
2 Katie	A	21–25	Degree	White British / Irish	Nathan	4	Yes	1	Lives with Nathan's father	£24,000–£41,999
3 Hannah	A	36+	Postgraduate	White British / Irish	Sidney	3	No	2	Lives with Sidney's father	More than £42,000
4 Laura	A	31–35	Degree	White British / Irish	Alex	3	Yes	1	Lives with Alex's father who is of Asian heritage	More than £42,000
5 Rebecca	B	36+	Degree	White British / Irish	Oliver	4	Yes	1	Lives with Oliver's father	£14,001 to £24,000
6 Tania	B	26–30	5+ GCSEs	White British / Irish	Ethan	3	Yes	1	Lone parent	Less than £14,000
7 Natalie	B	26–30	1–4 GCSEs	White British / Irish	Matthew	3	No	2	Natalie is a lone parent; the children have regular contact with their father	Less than £14,000

(continued)

55

Table 4.1 Cont.

Name	Cohort	Age	Qualifications	Ethnicity	Child's name	Child age	Is this first child?	Number of children	Household composition	Household income bracket
8 Sumaira	A	31–35	No formal qualifications	Asian British	Asha	3	No	2	Lives with Asha's father	Less than £14,000
9 Amy	B	26–30	1–4 GCSEs	White British / Irish	Maddie	3	Yes	1	Lives with Maddie's stepfather; Maddie visits father weekly	Less than £14,000
10 Kylie	B	31–35	No formal qualifications	White British / Irish	Brady	3	No	2	Lives with Brady's father	£14,001 to £24,000.
11 Victoria	A	36+	Postgraduate	White British / Irish	Greg	3	Yes	2	Lives with Greg's father and their newborn son	More than £42,000
12 Lisa	B	26–30	5+ GCSEs	White British / Irish	Georgina	4	No	3	Lives with her children's father; has a primary school aged child and a newborn baby. Her 4-year-old niece and nephew permanently live with the family.	£14,001 to £24,000

13	Bina	A	31–35	Degree	Asian British	Hadara	3	Yes	1	Lives with Hadara's father	£24,000–£41,999
14	Elizabeth	A	31–35	Postgraduate	White British / Irish	Leo	3	Yes	2	Lives with the children's father	More than £42,000
15	Fiona	A	31–35	GCSE	White British / Irish	Leila	4	Yes	1	Lives with Leila's father	£14,000–£24,000
16	Javid (father)	A	36+	GCSE	Pakistani British	Karim	3	No	3	Lives with his wife, adult son and primary school aged son	£14,000–£24,000
17	Latika	A	31–35	Postgraduate	Indian	Jasna	3	Yes	1	Lives with Jasna's father	£24,000–£41,999
18	Cathy	A	31–35	A-Level	White British/ Irish	Sophie	3	No	3	Lives with her husband	£14,000–£24,000
19	Sarah	A	36+	Data not collected	Mixed White British and Black British	Benjamin	3	No	3	Lives with two of her four children	Less than £14,000
20	Mia	A	31–35	Degree	Pakistani British heritage and children were mixed white and Asian British	Ali	3	No	2	Lives with her husband and two sons	Less than £14,000

(continued)

Table 4.1 Cont.

Name	Cohort	Age	Qualifications	Ethnicity	Child's name	Child age	Is this first child?	Number of children	Household composition	Household income bracket
21 Amal	A	36+	GCSE equivalent	Amal is Palestinian and her children Palistinian/British	Aisha	3	No	3	Lives with her husband and three children	Less than £14,000
22 Roshana	A	36+	Degree	Roshana was Iranian and her daughter was Iranian British	Karina	3	Yes	2	Lives with her husband and two children	Less than £14,000
23 Zainab	A	31–35	Data not collected	Pakistani British	Malima	1 year, 9 months	Yes	1	Lives with her husband	£14,000–£24,000
24 Tara	A	21–25	NVQ Level 3	Mixed heritage including Black British, White British	Archie	4	No	3		Less than £14,000

25	Farah	A	31–35	Degree	Farah was Iranian and her daughter was British Iranian	Laila	3	Yes	1	Lives with her husband	£14,000–£24,000
26	Jo	A	36+	Postgraduate	White British/Irish	Ellie	4	No	1	Lives with partner and two children	£24,000–£41,999
27	Kerry	B	31–35	5+ GCSEs	White British/Irish	Sarah	4	No	2	Lives with her husband and two children	Less than £14,000
28	Allison	B	26–30	A levels/NVQ Level 3	White British/Irish	Maeva	4	Yes	2	Lives with her husband and two children	More than £42,000
29	Elaine	B	31–35	1–4 GCSEs	White British/Irish	Phoebe	3	No	4	Lives with her 4 children	Less than £14,000

However, Gregory and Ruby also show how being an 'insider' can also raise dilemmas for researchers. Ruby reports her experiences as a researcher within the same population as Gregory; however, Ruby describes herself as a Bangladeshi and a Muslim. She talks about the fact that she entered the research with a desire to 'empower voices' within what she describes as a 'traditionally marginalized community' (169); however, she came to learn that some research participants were not willing to share their stories as they felt that she was 'being "used" to "gather" information to "expose" the community' (169). Even though Ruby reported that she felt like an 'insider', she concluded:

> I still had to build trust and confidence between myself and the participants similar to being an 'Outsider' because I am entering as an ethnographer into a 'protective' area of a family and their lives. (169–170)

We were largely 'outsiders' to most of the families in our study. In many cases we differed from the families in terms of culture and ethnicity, but to varying degrees we also differed from some families in terms of our educational background. This was a serious issue for consideration given that, as we mentioned earlier, reading is a value-laden construct and it is not unusual for people to feel judged about their reading. It was therefore critical to the study that we built trust with our participants; this was aided by a few strategies. Firstly as explained earlier in this chapter, we ensured that the interviews were designed in such a way as to allow participants to talk freely about their daily lives and family practices and routines. In some cases we were about forty-five minutes into the interview before we even started asking questions about reading. Secondly, we made sure that we spoke specifically to participants about the fact that our intention was not to assess, measure or judge their reading, or the reading they did with their children, but we wanted to *understand* aspects of their family lives and the role of reading within.

The other factors that supported the development of trust between researcher and participant related to the conduct of the two research assistants who were involved in the study. Jenny began working on the study first, having just completed her own Ph.D. Her own doctoral research had focused on decision-making practices in low-income households, which meant that she was well practiced in talking to people in their homes about aspects of their everyday lives. Jenny also had a young child who was a similar age to the target children in the study, so this also helped in establishing a rapport between the researcher and the participant. Jenny was also involved in the recruitment of all participants from Dalton. As explained earlier, recruitment was a lengthy process that involved Jenny's participation at many different children's groups; this meant that Jenny had already established relationships with the participants before the interviews, and trust was already apparent between the two parties.

Jenny went on maternity leave at about the mid-point of this three-year study, and Mel (the second author of this book) became the second research assistant to work on the project. Like Jenny, Mel had completed her own doctoral research; however, she had also worked on several other research projects. Mel brought a background in sociology to the study, which has informed the research in a variety of ways. However, Mel also came to the study with experience of interviewing young people about their experiences of living with a parent who has young onset dementia. This again demanded a great deal of sensitivity within the researcher–interviewer relationship and Mel was highly skilled in interviewing participants under these conditions. In brief, both Jenny and Mel were able to employ sensitive and sophisticated interview skills, which allowed participants to talk freely about their daily lives.

The participants appeared to feel comfortable with the research and seemed to enjoy being interviewed. Interview transcripts were punctuated with laughter, conversations with children and anecdotes. In general, it appeared that participants enjoyed having an opportunity to talk about their lives and experiences, their children, their concerns and their hopes for the future. Each interview took its own course, and participants shared experiences of their own childhoods, their own journeys into parenthood and their relationships with family and friends. Given the complexity of family life, we were witness to stories of sadness and loss as well as joy and hope. All of this was cemented into a picture of the everyday ways in which reading, and shared reading activity, featured in their own lives and the lives of their children.

The ethical implications of our positionality as researchers entering the private space of participants' homes, was a major consideration within this study; however, this was by no means the only ethical issue to consider. We made sure that participants were fully informed about our plans for the use of their data, including plans for publication, and that consent was given for this. We also ensured that all identifying information was removed from reports and publications and that pseudonyms would be used at all times. In addition, we felt that it was ethical that the participants should receive some direct benefit from taking part in the research, beyond the shopping voucher they received in return for their participation. We therefore planned a large dissemination event in the final month of the project, where all participants (including those taking part in the other studies) were invited to attend a session, in Dalton, with their children. This event was threefold, offering professional development for practitioners working with families, and activities for members of the general public, alongside an invited session for all research participants. This session included a story-based activity, a brief overview of salient findings from the studies, refreshments and the gifting of a goody bag; the goody bag included a children's book, small gifts, information about reading activities in the families' area and advice on how to promote and enjoy shared reading in the home. The whole event was extremely well attended with several hundred families attending the invited sessions.

Analysing the data

The interviews were audio recorded on a digital recording device and then transcribed verbatim by the member of the research team who had carried out the interview. Given the exploratory nature of this study, and the fact that little is known about the ways in which shared reading operates in families, we had to choose an analytical framework that allowed us to simultaneously reduce and manage the data, while also allowing for unforeseen findings to emerge. We recognised that themes do not simply 'emerge' from the data, and that analysis is an active process requiring deep engagement with the data (Braun & Clarke, 2013). Once transcription was complete, data were analysed in three stages: open coding, clustering of codes around categories and thematic coding (Braun & Clarke, 2006). Open coding and thematic coding were conducted by three researchers independently (Rachael, Jenny and Mel). In each case, transcripts were read, and re-read, and each researcher identified themes based on the research aims and questions. We then compared the resulting themes; there was substantial consistency among the researchers, which we took to signify that our themes were valid. We then worked together to develop a 'final' set of codes; however, given the cyclical and recursive nature of this research, we engaged in further stages of data analysis for quite some time. For example, having identified links between parents' own reading and the shared reading they engaged in with their children, we began to notice that there was a subset of parents in this sample who identified themselves as being 'non-readers', or reported that they disliked reading, but who went on to have strong shared reading relationships with their own children. This discovery provoked a fresh cycle of data analysis in order to try to understand this further.

We developed a number of codes during the first few cycles of data analysis, which were:

- Parents' perspectives on school
- Parents' experiences of reading as a child (including being read to)
- Parents' reading as an adult
- Shared reading relationship with child
- Siblings
- How parents and children read together

- Daily routines
- Bedtime routines
- Technology
- Access to books
- Parents' perceptions of value of shared reading
- Cultural and ethnicity
- Role of gender
- Extended family
- Responsibility and guilt
- Outside authorities (e.g. health visitors, teachers)
- Reading to babies
- Play
- Religion
- Future aspirations for child.

In some cases, a code was sufficient to use through the whole process of the analysis; however, in other cases, codes needed to be refined and developed. For example, 'Parents' experiences of reading as a child' did not support the complexity of parents' own reading as a child and required the code to be expanded to include:

- Parent reading with own parents
- Parent reading to self as a child
- Parent reading at school
- Parents' views of schooled reading.

Conclusion

Previous research into shared reading in homes has tended to focus on the ways in which family reading practices support children's language development, but very little research has attempted to understand the factors that motivate or inhibit shared reading activity in the home. Given the urgent need for research that talks to parents about their everyday lives and seeks to understand how shared reading may, or may not fit within this, this chapter has presented an overview of the methods used to design a study that has explored shared reading in families by talking to participants in their own homes about this. It has also given an overview of some of the issues and complexities that arise when designing research to explore participants' lived experiences, along with description of the measures we took in this study to address these.

Recognising that narrative methods can be 'productive in providing a picture of how people "do", "display" and commemorate family practices over time' (Phoenix & Brannen, 2014: 22), this study has encouraged parents of young children to talk about the stories of their everyday lives, as well as past experiences and perspectives, in order to shine light on the ways in which shared reading features in homes, and explain why parents do, and do not read with their children. The following chapters now report the findings from this study beginning with the ways in which shared reading operated as an everyday practice in homes.

5

SHARED READING AS AN EVERYDAY FAMILY PRACTICE

Introduction

Previous chapters have shown how the ways in which individuals have come to understand the construct of 'reading', and indeed 'shared reading', are embedded in discourses of power and authority and are shaped by the various systems within which a person resides. We argued in Chapter 2 that perceptions of reading continue to be dominated by the school discourse, despite the fact that we also know that the home environment is critical in supporting children's literacy and language development in different ways (Griffin & Morrison, 1997; Park, 2008; Brown et al., 2013). Given that shared reading has particular benefits for children (Bus et al., 1995; Mol et al., 2008), it is important to understand how shared reading operates within families, yet very little is known about the ways in which it is constructed, developed and practiced in homes. This is especially true of shared reading with young children, which has tended to be researched from the perspective of 'educational endeavour', rather than understanding what it is, how it functions within families and what families gain from the practice.

The Shared Reading Project was designed to enable parents to talk in detail about their lives with their young children and discuss the motivators and barriers to shared reading within the context of everyday family life. Data from this study indicates that shared reading occupies a significant role in these families' lives. This, and the following three chapters explore how shared reading functions as an everyday practice in homes, what motivates parents to read with their children, what parents need in order to begin or sustain shared reading activity in the home, the factors that act as barriers to shared reading and the ways in which parents' own reading relationships connect with their shared reading practices with their children. This present chapter begins with an insight into what shared reading is for these families and how it forms part of everyday family practices (Morgan, 1996), how it is used to display aspects of family life (Finch, 2007) and what shared reading does for the family. The chapter closes with a brief look at the materials that families use within their shared reading activity.

Shared reading in everyday family life

For many of the families in this study, shared reading was part of their everyday lives and everyday family practices. Just as other researchers have found that the routine practices of events such as mealtimes can support the organisation of family life (Fiese, 2006), data from the Shared Reading Project reveal that shared reading was not only part of daily family routines, but plays a major role in *establishing* family routines. Given that previous research has described shared reading as the lynchpin of the bedtime routine for families (Nichols, 2000), it was not surprising to find that it featured in many of the bedtime routines within this study. Zainab (Dalton cohort: lives with her husband and daughter aged 1 year and 9 months), for example, recounted her daughter's bedtime and reported that the bedtime story was critical to this:

> She has a bath in the evening ... she likes to watch a few nursery rhymes on the tablet and I'll read her a story. She's got so many books, I read her a story and that's it ... once she's finished her bottle ....

Similarly Hadra (Dalton cohort: lives with her husband, three-year-old daughter and son of high school age) told us that she and her husband only incorporated reading 'into a routine' so that their daughter 'would know bath, book, bed' and therefore 'identify that it's bedtime – to get her into a routine'. This notion of using shared reading to establish an effective bedtime routine was also described in detail by Katie (Dalton cohort: lives with her husband and 4-year-old son) who reported:

> We got the routine established really early – bath, story, bed ... he was eight weeks old and I remember one night going 'I need to get a routine, I just can't do this random kind of going to sleep when he's ready ... we need to get his routine sorted out'.

This data is demonstrating that shared reading at night was not just part of the bedtime routine but was instrumental in creating the routine. In fact, several parents went on to suggest that if shared reading did not happen, then bedtimes would be disrupted. For example, having stated that the main reason for reading to her children at night was because it was simply 'something we do before bedtime', Hannah (Dalton cohort: lives with her husband, her 3-year-old son and another son of primary school age) went on to say that if they did not read with their children they (the children) would 'pick up that the routine had changed and they would act differently'. Similarly, Laura (Dalton cohort: lives with her husband and their 3-year-old son) made the statement 'I don't think anyone would sleep if we didn't have books', again highlighting the role of shared reading in establishing an effectual bed-time routine.

Many of the parents in this project valued shared reading because it provided an opportunity for them to spend protected time with their children and enjoy being close to their child. This is evidenced repeatedly within the next few chapters and is illustrated in Allison's (Barnwell cohort: lives with her husband and daughter aged 3 years 8 months and a son just 6 months old) interview. Allison, who was on maternity leave with her youngest child at the time of the interview, shared how she enjoyed reading to her children at the end of the day and was saddened by the anticipation that this would change at the end of her leave. She reported:

> It's good to have the one to one and the wind down time with them. It's not going to be as easy when I go back to work because I'm going to be at work until six o clock so it's going to be my Mum doing the bed time routine on those days, and I'll find it hard because I won't get that little bit of time before she goes to bed. I like that.

As we went further into the data, it became increasingly clear that the various ways in which parents used shared reading as a vehicle to spend time with their children were specific to the everyday lives, routines and practices of individual families. This was often seen in relation to the ways in which parents, within two-parent families, decided who was going to read a bedtime story to their child(ren). For example, Allison reported that her husband tended not to be involved with shared reading because of his nightshift working pattern, which meant that he simply was not around when their child was going to bed. In other families, where both parents were around in the evening, shared reading was often conducted primarily by one of the two parents. Cathy (Dalton cohort: lives with her husband and daughters aged 3 years and 6 years and 11-year-old son) tended to lead shared reading, with her husband taking over 'only if I'm feeling poorly, or ill ... if I'm feeling poorly then my husband will go right, come on, let's go to bed early, I'll read you some books in bed'. In other households where the mother was at home during the day, there was a deliberate decision for the father to read in the evening, so that he could spend some 'quality' time with the child(ren). This was seen in Victoria's (Dalton cohort: lives with her partner and their two sons, aged 3 years old and a baby under a year old) interview; Victoria was on maternity leave at the time and spoke of being at home with her son while her husband was at work. She felt that she had the opportunity to bond with her son during the day and that shared reading at bedtime afforded her husband the chance for this too. She told us:

> Because my husband works really long hours and I'm on mater-nity leave, I've got more time during the day, so at night-time, my

husband reads the stories ... he wants to and he wants to spend time
with him.

This shows that these parents were using shared reading to cement routine
into their everyday family lives. However, the practice of shared reading was
providing more than just a routine – parents were using the practice as an
opportunity to spend protected time with their child, to nurture their relationship and promote bonding. Indeed, some families were clearly taking this
into consideration when making decisions about which parent would read
with the child(ren).

While it was common to find that shared reading was used to ensure a
routine at bedtime, it was apparent that families used shared reading at
other times of the day too. For example, Kylie (Barnwell cohort: lives with
her husband and two children: a son aged 3 and a daughter aged 11 years
old) stated that she tended to read with her son during the day 'just because
his books are out'. Other parents spoke of embedding shared reading into
daytime routines in order to manage aspects of family life. This was particularly evident in Kerry's (Barnwell cohort: lives with her husband and two
children – a 3-year-old daughter and a son of primary school age) interview.
Kerry spoke of finding it difficult to read with her younger daughter, because
the presence of her older son, who has autism, could make it hard for the
younger daughter to engage in shared reading. Kerry therefore developed
a routine of reading with her daughter when her son was at Nursery. She
told us:

> I do try and do it of an afternoon while it's just me and her because
> sometimes when Noah goes off and walks away ... you can see her
> losing a little bit of interest ... because Noah's walked away ... I do
> find it difficult when there's two of them there.

What we are seeing here is that in addition to having a role in the development of routine, many of the families in this study also used shared reading
as a tool in the management of everyday family life. This was evident across
the data; for example, one parent described how she would sit and read with
her son while potty training him, as a way of making the training more enjoyable. Other parents spoke of using shared reading as way of occupying a
younger child, when older children in the family were engaged with extra-
curricular activities. For example, Jo (Dalton cohort: lives with her partner
and two daughters – the youngest aged 4 and the oldest of primary school
age) reported:

> We'll be doing after school things with her sister, like going to watch
> her go swimming and then if I was doing that, I'd always take books
> or something to play with.

Parents also told us that they used shared reading as a reward, or the withdrawal of shared reading as a punishment, in order to encourage desirable behaviour from their children. Given that the children appeared to really enjoy shared reading, it was interesting to note how some parents used the activity to promote certain behaviour in their child. For example, Tania (Barnwell cohort: lives with her 3-year-old son) said, 'I use it like a reward system. Now if he's been naughty in the day, I'll tell him "it's your bedtime story" ... it works'. In other data Jo told us how she used shared reading as a treat to be used to reward her daughter for good behaviour when she said, 'It's totally a tool ... I could literally bribe her with reading a book, she likes them that much'.

Other parents spoke of using books to help manage aspects of family life with small children, even though they were not actually reading the books with their children. Victoria, for example, spoke of giving her son books when he was in the car, which helped to occupy him during her drive to work each morning. Similarly, Kylie told us how she used books to entertain her son during the weekly supermarket shop. Speaking of purchasing books she stated:

> We get loads from [the supermarket] because when we go shopping, the easiest thing to do is to go to the book aisle, let him pick a book, sit him in the trolley and then I can do my shopping ... I can throw everything in the trolley while he's concentrating.

Kylie's interview also showed how in the management of everyday family life, shared reading appeared to afford opportunities for parents to work with their children in ways that allowed them to play to their strengths. Speaking of her husband, and the way in which he reads with their son, Kylie described how her husband entertained their son by putting on loud voices when reading, while she tended to read more calmly and quietly. Kylie was clear about the fact that these different approaches were complementary and achieved different outcomes, with her husband supporting the development of their son's imagination and interest, while her reading was more likely to 'settle' their son, and encourage him to 'get into his book'. Other parents reported that reading was more likely to be conducted with one parent or the other; for example, when Natalie (Barnwell cohort: lives with her two sons aged 8 and 3 years and 10 months) was asked if her son read with his father (with whom he did not live) she remarked that this was 'very rare, I think he [my son] sees it as our thing ... Dad's is football'. This again suggests that shared reading was used by some parents to assert a particular parenting role within the family, which was in turn used to manage aspects of family life such as entertaining or settling the children.

What we learned from the families in this study is that shared reading was not only part of their everyday family practices but had a role in developing routines and managing aspects of their daily lives. Shared reading was used to help the family to organise, structure and develop everyday activity. In other words, shared reading was not only a family practice, it was used as a tool to help manage aspects of parenting and life in general; it solidified routines, provided a space to develop relationships and helped parents to handle some of the complexities associated with the practical management of everyday family life. However, the data not only revealed what shared reading was within the context of these homes, it also provided an insight into what shared reading can do for families and the individuals within. This is discussed next in relation to the teaching and re-inscribing of family values and identities.

Using shared reading in families

As demonstrated above, families embedded shared reading into their daily lives to fulfil a number of different functions. Alongside this, we became increasingly aware that the families in the Shared Reading Project were also using shared reading to achieve certain goals and meet various family needs. Careful analysis of the data revealed that shared reading was being used as a tool to teach and socialise children within the family. In addition, shared reading also provided opportunities for families to 'display' (Finch, 2007) their agency and indeed 'familyness' to each other and the outside world. Together this showed that shared reading was used in various ways to impart values and present identities that were important to the individual family.

Parents in this study spoke about shared reading as an activity that was simply part of everyday child-rearing, given that it afforded opportunities for parents to teach their children. Sometimes the focus was on the skill of reading itself – for example, Natalie argued that 'reading is important – you teach your child to go to the toilet so you should teach them how to read'. Many others though spoke about shared reading as an opportunity to teach their children about things that were not necessarily related to a literacy discourse. For example, several parents talked about purchasing books for their children that had a story about toilet training, which they used to support the process of toilet training at home. Kerry spoke specifically about the value of books as a tool to support parents in educating their children about the world around them, when she stated that books do more than provide direct teaching. She continued:

> Some books have got like hidden messages in them … if he needs the dentist, get a book and that'll, you know, make them feel a bit more easier.

In this respect, parents were using the context of shared reading to support aspects of their parenting in general. This was also vividly apparent in relation to the teaching of values, where several parents reported that they used shared reading to support their endeavours to teach their children to behave in a certain way. Hannah described this in detail when she said:

> You can try and help them to see things from a different perspective without kind of saying 'you're right' or 'you're wrong' ... You know – 'remember in the book that we read about that...'. You can sort of depersonalise the situation but something that they're familiar with and might understand a bit more... When I look for books for Freddy, I'm looking for strong, positive role models. Like there's often naughty boys in Topsy and Tim and we'd kind of talk about it being bad and what you might do. You know – 'is that a good or bad thing to do?' or 'you wouldn't do that, you're a good boy at sharing aren't you?'.

The ways in which parents used books to teach their children about values and behaviour varied from family to family. As seen above, Hannah used books to create some distance between her own voice and her child, by focusing on the 'message' within the book, rather than the message coming from her as an authority over her child. Roshana (Dalton cohort: an Iranian woman who lives with her husband and their two children, their 3-year-old daughter and a son aged under 2 years old) took a different approach when she told us that she would substitute names in the story for her children's names, in an attempt to encourage her children to understand when they had been 'naughty'. By putting her children into the story, she tried to link the positive behaviour, or the adjustment to negative behaviour in the book, with her own children's behaviour, therefore encouraging them to 'be good'.

As well as using shared reading to support aspects of their everyday parenting, several parents spoke about their desire to use the activity to promote their children's growing identity as a *reader*. Some parents spoke of this in connection with gendered reading identities. For example, Victoria reported that as she currently had time with her son during the day, her husband reads stories to their son at night-time; however, she went on to express her feelings about this in the statement 'how powerful it is for him (her son) to have a male role model reading'. Kylie, on the other hand, spoke of her own adherence to gender stereotypes in relation to the activities she engaged in with her children. Speaking of her son, she reported:

> He's boisterous, everything is exciting and I'm just no good at that. My little girl – I can play Barbies with her. But him? Everything dies! I can't do that. The boys – they just do the boisterous thing, and I do the reading and the Play-Doh.

This excerpt from Kylie appears to be suggesting that reading is aligned with femininity, and this stereotypical construction is played out in her home; however, she is aware that this may disadvantage her son, who she would like to develop engagement with reading. She went on to say:

> I just want him to be confident to read. And with boys, because girls do enjoy sitting and reading, my little girl enjoys books, but I think once boys get older, they start losing it. They don't want to read books. I think boys tend to be a little bit slower than girls so that's why I push it.

In different ways, both Victoria and Kylie were trying to use shared reading to encourage their boys to develop their own identities as readers, given that they both believed that boys tend to be less engaged with reading in comparison with girls. In other interviews, parents spoke about identities of being 'a reader' developing within the family, which they associated with shared reading. Just as previous research has shown that the identification of family resemblances can help individuals to feel connected to loved ones (Davies and Mason, 2008; Mason, 2008), some parents in the Shared Reading project spoke of a strong reading identity as being something that children could almost inherit from their parents. For example, Kerry drew parallels between her daughter and her husband when she said, 'I do think she'd enjoy them [books] when she's older ... Her Dad's like that. Her Dad will sit and read, he's got books and books'. Similarly, Amal (Dalton cohort: lives with her husband and three of their children including a 3-year-old daughter, a daughter of primary school age and an 18-year-old son; she also has two older children who no longer live with her; Amal is Palestinian and her children Palestinian British) argued that her daughter would probably continue to enjoy reading as an adult, because she herself was an avid reader. Amal reported: 'I like too much reading ... I know my daughter – why she reads, because she has genes. You take from your family'.

As the data has shown, parents in this study used shared reading as part of their everyday parenting practices, to teach their children about values and to instil aspects of identity that were important to their individual family. In connection with this, the data also indicated that shared reading provided an opportunity for both children and parents to exert agency in various ways. It was particularly evident, across most of the interviews, that shared reading was often child-led; this is discussed in more detail in Chapter 6. To illustrate, like many of the other parents in the study, Javid (Dalton cohort: lives with his wife and three sons one of whom is over 18 years, one is of primary school age and one is 3 years old) told us that it was his son who 'got the ball rolling' with shared reading by bringing books to him – and it was not 'the other way round'. Similarly, Kylie stated that they read 'just because his (her son's) books are out and he'll just go and get them'.

Given that previous research has indicated that children play an active role in their own socialisation and the construction of their own identities (James, 2013), this suggests that shared reading can provide a context for children to enact their emerging agency. This was evident in the data in a whole variety of ways. For example, Laura reported that her son knew all his books 'off by heart' and 'corrects you if you get it wrong' when she read these books to him. Latika (Dalton cohort: lives with her husband and their 3-year-old daughter) told us that her daughter would take ownership over who read with her; speaking of her daughter Latika stated, 'Sometimes she will say "Papa can you read it? I don't want Mama, I want you", sometimes she say, "I don't want Papa, I want Mama".' In these cases, it was apparent that shared reading activity provided an opportunity for the child to take control and exert agency. What is more, parents appeared to be aware of this and were keen to support their child's autonomy. In other cases, parents were seen to be actively facilitating their child's agency within the context of reading activity. This was evident when Elizabeth (Dalton cohort: lives with her husband and two sons, one aged 2 years and another under a year old) described the way she used reading to encourage her son to take more ownership of his own bedtime. She reported:

> Sometimes he's not quite ready to go to sleep, and I say to him, 'Have a look at the book for a minute by yourself then, and I'll go downstairs, and then when you've finished, put the book down and go to sleep.' And sometimes I can see him looking through the pages by himself. Again, that's a fairly new thing that he's kind of been willing to do, to sort of put himself to sleep in that way and use the book as a way of extending his bedtime.

Interestingly though, the data revealed that shared reading not only had benefits for children in terms of identity formation and agency, but also supported parents in aspects of their own identity formation. In order to understand this it is useful to return to the work of Finch (2007), introduced in Chapter 2, who argued that the concept of 'family display' exists because it allows families to provide evidence to their own members, and the outside world, that they are 'doing' family and demonstrating that 'this is my family and it works' (2007: 73). This could be seen in several of the interviews. For example, Bina (Dalton cohort: lives with her husband and their 3-year-old daughter), who had struggled to conceive, reported that she started reading to her daughter almost as soon as she was born, because she wanted to be performing parent–child activities which helped her to affirm her role as a mother. She reported, 'I just felt it was like a comfort thing for me. I enjoyed it, you know. It was nice to know I've got a little baby of my own and I'm reading to her.'

Bina was here describing how she was using shared reading to display her motherhood to herself, which was something that she found both comforting

73

and enjoyable. In other data, we found that shared reading was being used to display a notion of 'familyness'. Amy (Barnwell cohort: lives with her partner and her daughter aged 4 years from a previous relationship) had separated from her daughter's father and had recently moved in with her new partner. In the extract below, Amy describes the way that her boyfriend reads with her daughter, emphasising the role this plays in the cultivation of this 'new' family unit.

> Most of the time, it's my boyfriend [who reads]. He's much better and she laughs more when he does it – he's got better voices. She would like 10 books and is 'right let's go' ... She's excited, she loves it. I think as well, her Dad doesn't do anything like that ... so she looks at Jamie (her boyfriend) as... I don't want to say 'as Dad' but he looks at her as his own daughter.

What is so revealing about this quote is the way that Amy is recognising that the shared reading taking place between her partner and her daughter is a symbol of 'doing family' (Morgan, 1996). In describing the way that Jamie reads with her daughter, Amy is drawn to mention that the relationship between her daughter and her boyfriend resembles that of father and daughter. In other words, it appears that shared reading offers an opportunity for individuals to display being 'a family' – regardless of the technicalities of the connection.

So far in this chapter we have shown how shared reading can serve many different functions in families. In this section we have demonstrated how it can be used to support parenting in various ways such as to impart values and to solidify identities. The next section looks more closely at one particular function of shared reading activity within the family, and that is the way in which it facilitates opportunities for parents to be physically close with their child.

Shared reading and physical connections

Previous research has identified that shared reading is associated with physical closeness, as the activity encourages the parent and child to enjoy being in close proximity with one another; for example, as discussed in the introduction, Audet et al. (2008) found that parents reported that their goals for shared reading included bonding with their child. Other studies have stated that there is an association between shared reading and 'attachment' (Frosch et al., 2001), with the underlying suggestion that shared reading is beneficial in facilitating 'secure' parent–child attachment. While this may well be the case for some families, findings from our study indicate that shared reading activity is not just a vehicle for promoting connections when attachment between child and parent is described in some quarters as being 'insecure', but is a window into the ways in which parents and children display intimacy and affection within the context of their everyday lives.

This connects vividly with the work of Mason (2008), who speaks about 'tangible affinities' in relation to the lived experience of 'kinship'. Mason identifies four 'dimensions of affinity', which operate within families, helping us to understand connection and relatedness, yet it is Mason's conceptualisation of 'sensory affinity' that resonates most closely with the shared reading interactions that parents described in their interviews. Mason (2008: 41–42) argues that sensory affinities are 'engaging, evocative and preoccupying', and as such 'constitute a major currency through which kinship is transacted and understood'. Building on the work of Strathern (2005), who speaks of the role of bodily connections in the manifestation of kinship, Mason goes on to state that kinship might present a 'distinctive set of ways of thinking about bodily connection', meaning that 'particular ideas or experiences of sensory relationality accompany affinities of kinship'.

Many of the parents in this study spoke freely about the embodied experiences of shared reading activity, which was linked with an intimate connection between parent and child. For example, in describing a typical shared reading interaction with her son, Katie told us:

> He normally sits on my lap really cuddly and he'll just sit there and he just sits very neat with his little hands like this, like crossed over, just on his lap. It's a very kind of close, bonding thing with him. He loves it, he just, he really enjoys it.

Hadra also provided a strong image of the embodied nature of shared reading activity. Having reported that her daughter used to 'read her book downstairs', Hadra went on to say that it was 'different' with her son because:

> He always needed his bedtime story in bed – we used to read it in bed with him. So his dad used to get into his single bed with him … he used to prefer it when his dad read his book, because they'd spend an hour reading a book.

Hadra and Katie both provide vivid images of a close embodied experience. Katie described the interaction during shared reading as being 'really cuddly', while painting an affectionate picture of her son's 'little hands' being crossed on his lap. Hadra also evoked a strong visual image of her husband and son lying close together in a 'single bed', which was clearly enjoyed by both father and son as the reading would last for 'an hour'.

The physical impact of shared reading was also emphasised by Victoria. When talking about the way shared reading was experienced in her home she stated:

I think it's just sort of a closer, a closer time, because you're sat down and it's quiet and you can snuggle in rather than being active. It's just different – it's just making sure your life's got all those different aspects in, so there's a time for being active and there's a time for being quiet.

Like Hadra and Katie, Victoria associates shared reading with not only being calm and quiet, but with an essence of closeness. The pleasure of an embodied shared experience with her son is evident in her words 'snuggle in' which again suggests that shared reading promotes an opportunity for parent and child to experience a sensory exchange. The role of the senses in shared reading activity is vastly under-explored; however, the data suggests that shared reading is a highly sensory experience, which may contribute towards its role in promoting intimacy between parent and child. In speaking about the role of the senses in connecting with others, Mason (2018: 7) argues that:

We sense others. We know what they are like and who they are by seeing, touching, smelling, hearing and generally experiencing the sensations of them, at the same time as they are experiencing the sensations of us.

Drawing on Mason's conceptualisation of 'sensory relationality', a concept that is particularly relevant to the interactions between family members, we start to understand how shared reading may offer an opportunity for a parent and child to experience a particular kind of embodied interaction that may not occur during other activities. This was especially evident in Tania's description of a shared reading encounter.

It's dead cuddle when he's doing it, like you seen before [when I was reading with him], he tried to climb on my knee, so it's always been like a bonding thing for us as well ... and *I can see him*, literally, it's like you can *see him taking it in*. But we both, we both gain from it, definitely, it's a good quality time ... a bit of me and him time. And like he knows he can run round all day, do you know what I mean, and dance and all that, but you know once you get them books out, especially for bedtime, it's our little time. You can turn the telly off, have *no background noise* and all that .... that was our little five minutes of *shush*, you know, just *a kiss and cuddle* and have our books and that, and he was really receptive to it, he really is.

Tania's account of shared reading with her son is portrayed as a highly sensory experience. She is seeing her son's face 'taking it (the story) in', she is hearing the 'five minutes of shush' and enjoying the escape from 'background noise', she is feeling the sensation of a 'kiss and a cuddle'. What we can see here is that shared reading provided an opportunity for an intimate display of affection between parent and child, characterised by a sensory exchange. Other parents also spoke of their shared reading interactions in terms of a sensory connection. Kylie reported that she particularly likes to read to her son at night 'because he's all bathed and fresh and I can get in bed with him and things', going on to say 'if I don't read then I don't get in bed with him' which is 'nice and cosy'.

What we are seeing here is that for many of the families in this study, shared reading can facilitate a special physical connection between parent and child. These parents are describing an encounter that goes beyond accepted constructions of 'attachment'. By drawing on Mason's conceptu- alisation of *affinity*, and the role of the senses in promoting connections between people, and family members in particular, we begin to appreciate that shared reading can be a highly sensory activity. This helps to explain why shared reading can be so powerful in supporting the development of a bond between parent and child, in comparison with other family practices and everyday activities.

So far, we have discussed the various ways in which shared reading operated within these families. In relation to the context of everyday family life, we have explored *why* shared reading happens and *what it does* for families, but we have not yet considered *what resources* are being used during shared reading events. This is discussed next.

Shared reading: what is being read

Even though we were careful to make sure that the parents in this study were able to talk about all the different kinds of texts that they may have shared with their children, including those on screen as well as paper-based texts, most of the parents spoke about sharing paper-based books with their children. This was not terribly surprising given that research has suggested that even though digital texts are widely used in homes (Marsh et al., 2005; Carrington & Robinson, 2009) much of the reading that takes place between young children and their parents still involves the use of books (Dickinson, 2001; Denney et al., 2010).

There was no doubt that many of the parents in this study spoke very warmly and positively about the books that they shared with their young children. Many of the parents told us that their children 'loved books' and that they featured strongly in the fabric of everyday life. Within the sample as a whole, parents told us that they bought books for their children online, in the supermarket and in bookstores. Several parents reported that the first books they acquired for their children were from the health visitor. Books were also handed down in families and passed on by friends, while some parents also spoke about 'recycling' books that they had had as children themselves. Not surprisingly these books were often spoken about with great nostalgia, which in turn had implications for parents' perceptions of reading with their children – this is discussed in more detail in Chapter 7.

Books were also borrowed from schools and local libraries. Comments in relation to the use of a local library were particularly valuable in helping us to understand how shared reading featured as an everyday practice for some of these families. To illustrate, a few parents spoke about the integration of regular trips to the library as being part of their weekly routine. For example, Hadra told us that her husband's excursions with their daughter would often include a visit to 'the library, and then they will go to the pet shop'. Elizabeth also reported that she would often take her daughter to *Babytime*, which took place at 'the central library at quarter past even on Fridays' and involved singing and 'looking at books in the library'.

The act of going to the library provided these parents with an opportunity to conduct an activity with their children away from the home, although Elizabeth also reported that going to the library was 'nice' because she then has access to 'a whole load of books that we don't have', which she appreciated because she does 'get bored reading the same things with him (her son) over and over and over and over'. Interestingly, this contrasted with Tania's initial response to the question of going to the library when she stated that she used to think 'I'm not going to take him to the library when I've got a pile of books at home'; however, Tania went on to describe how her views changed once she started taking her son to the library. She reported:

> When we went in there, he was in there for about two hours – couldn't get out of it! Loved it! Loved it – because the way it's laid out. It's got all comfy bits for reading. And he's 'Read this one!', I think I read about four or five of them before we even left. But as I say, it killed a Sunday afternoon for us. You know what I mean – cheap and cheerful.

Together this suggests that parents may value the library as a resource in itself – a place where parent and child can enjoy passing time, as well as having the opportunity to read new books. However, other parents told us that they were not comfortable in borrowing books from the library for their children. Farah (Dalton cohort: British Iranian; lived with her husband and their 3-year-old daughter), for example, was worried that library books would be 'dirty', so she preferred to own books rather than borrow them. Bina's concern about borrowing library books was very different. She told us that she had joined a library and got her daughter her own library card; however, once she had borrowed books and brought them home she became

78

'scared' that her daughter may damage the books. She came to the conclusion that she would rather 'just have books where I'm not worried if she writes on them, or tears them', which meant that she did not want to be 'dealing with the library'.

What we learn from this is that even in this 'digital age' (Merchant, 2007), books continue to feature strongly within the practice of shared reading in families. As demonstrated in this chapter, and indeed in many of the chapters to follow, the books that parents and children share together are valued and enjoyed, but above all they are *used* within the context of everyday family life. While it is fair to say that most of the time parents in this study spoke about books in hard copy, when discussing shared reading practices, it was clear from the data that texts in a whole variety of formats were shared with children.

There were occasions when parents spoke about using digital texts with their children. For example, Farah told us that her daughter sometimes 'doesn't like books' but does enjoy using 'the iPad and mobile phone'. She went on to say that 'the iPad's very good' because through using the tablet, her daughter 'can now read the alphabet' and when they are in the street her daughter is 'trying to read the street name'. This shows how Farah's daughter was clearly engaged with her reading on the iPad, evident in the fact that she was able to connect her reading on the iPad (where she was learning to read the alphabet) to a different domain (the street) where she was trying to read environmental print. Farah was not the only parent to report that she read digital texts with her child. Other parents spoke about sharing 'nursery rhyme books that came with CDs' (Tara: Dalton cohort: lives with her husband and three children aged 2, 4 and 8 years old), sharing books that come in 'tablet form' (Cathy, Dalton cohort: lives with her husband and three children aged 3, 6 and 11 years), sharing stories (Tania) and cartoons (Amy) on the mobile phone, watching television programmes together (Amal, Latika, Elizabeth) and using audio books (Cathy).

What is more, when talking about shared reading, several of the parents in this study naturally started talking about oral storytelling. For example, having spoken about the fact that her daughter tended to ask many questions during shared book reading, Latika described how she found it more engaging, and less frustrating, to make up her own stories to tell her daughter. Latika stated:

> I made one story for her – a hunter story. I just came like, once upon a time there was a hunter, he goes to a forest and he was looking for some birds. The she (daughter) said, 'but he only looks for a baby birds Moma, not all birds!'. I said 'ok, baby birds then'. Then she said, 'because my bird's gonna protect her' and I said 'ok', so she knows. The she says 'Mummy, all the elder's gonna protect the

younger', so she said 'so the hunter's only gonna pick the baby ones, not the Mummy or Papa, or, like, any older ones.

Similarly, Cathy also spoke about making up stories with her children. Interestingly, throughout her interview, Cathy spoke about her commitment to helping her daughter 'to develop her understanding of the actual story, so she's not just reading the words'. This may have explained why she was so keen on creating oral stories with her children. She went on to talk about occasions when she would make up stories with her children, such as:

> We're quite creative. If I just randomly go 'once upon a time there was a little boy', and then my daughter will finish the next thing, and then we'll start just creating a story together.

Cathy also told us that sometimes they 'could just get the salt and pepper pot and kind of just make up a story', or sometimes they would make up stories 'walking home from school, or we do it walking to school'. Cathy went on to tell us that she believed that children 'naturally learn and develop through play', going on to emphasise that 'play hasn't always got to be a physical toy in front of you' but can be 'skipping down the road, it can be singing silly songs, it can be reading'.

When we bring all of this together it suggests that rather than focusing on *what* was being read during the shared reading interactions that occurred in this study, it is more fruitful to focus on *what was happening* during the events. As will become increasingly evident in the next few chapters, the project data revealed that shared reading practices were highly individual and unique to the social and cultural context of the family. How parents read with their children was strongly connected to their motivations for reading and the ways in which they read.

Conclusion

This chapter has shown that for the families in this study, shared reading was not only part of their everyday family practice but had a role in structuring and managing aspects of family life. It was also clear that shared reading supported the act of parenting in various ways, as it was used to help impart values and solidify identities, as well as support the more practical elements of parenting such as cementing routines. By drawing on Mason's (2018) concept of affinities, and exploring the role of the senses in promoting connections between people, it became clear that as shared reading is a highly sensory activity, it can also play a vital role in supporting the development of a bond between parent and child.

In conclusion, while some parents did talk about reading with their children for reasons of educational endeavour, the data strongly indicate that shared reading offered far more than this, and was, for many, an invaluable component of everyday family life. This raises important questions about parents' own motivations for reading with their children. The next chapter addresses this by looking specifically at what appeared to motivate the parents in this study to read with their children, reflecting on what parents need in order to begin or sustain shared reading activity in the home.

6

DOING AND SUSTAINING SHARED READING; PARENTS' AIMS AND MOTIVATIONS

As demonstrated in the previous chapter, this study suggests that shared reading is an everyday practice in some families and contributes towards the pool of activities that make up everyday family life. However, this does not mean that parents do not have their own aims and motivations for reading with their children. Indeed, the parents in this study reported a variety of different aims and motivations for reading with their children and these are presented in this chapter. Understanding what motivated these parents to read with their children is important as it not only helps us to understand why parents may choose to read with their children, but also shines light on what they need in order to begin or sustain shared reading activity. Beginning with a focus on the role of enjoyment, this chapter explores what motivates parents, why they choose to read to their children and – as a consequence of this – what they need in order to begin or sustain shared reading activity in the home.

The role of enjoyment

Almost all of the parents in this study spoke spontaneously about the enjoyment of shared reading activity. Parents spoke at length about their children enjoying being read to, but they also talked about their enjoyment in reading to their children. This is not a surprise given that previous research has shown that while parents have different goals for shared reading, it is the goals of enjoying reading and bonding with their children that are rated most highly by parents (Audet et al., 2008). However, it is important to understand what 'enjoying shared reading' really means for both child and adult, especially if we are to use this understanding to support parents who may not have developed enjoyable shared reading relationships with their children.

To begin, parents talked about enjoying the atmosphere that emanated from the activity, with many of the parents in the project using words such as 'calm', 'cosy' and 'relaxing' when describing their shared reading interactions. For example Lisa (Barnwell cohort: lives with her husband and two children – a daughter aged 4 and a son aged 8) reported that she had 'always read' to her children 'since they were babies' and this was usually an enjoyable thing to do. When asked about her motivations for reading, Lisa stated, 'to be honest it's quite relaxing, to go up to her room with her and read a book'. Similarly, Fiona (Dalton cohort: lives with her husband and 4-year-old daughter) talked in detail about the importance of her daughter's bedtime routine which included a bedtime story. Having previously told us that her daughter was 'just not interested' in being read to when she was under the age of 2, Fiona reported that 'it just wouldn't be possible now' to take her to bed without a story. However, Fiona seemed to enjoy the routine as much as her daughter, evident in her words, 'it's just that nice time together, just you two, it's quiet and you can just relax and read that story together'.

While these parents were both specific about shared reading being 'relaxing', other parents expressed similar sentiments. Tara spoke of the pleasure of reading nursery rhymes to her children because 'they are calming', while Elizabeth said that she and her husband would take time to settle their son at night and enjoy spending time 'reading with him and getting it all calm and everything'. Several other parents also spoke about shared reading being an activity associated with 'calmness', and in many cases this was also associated with bonding. For example, Rebecca (Barnwell cohort: lives with her partner and son aged 3 years and 11 months) reported that one of the main differences between shared reading and other shared activities was that she found reading 'calm'. She went on to point out:

> Life isn't always calm with a three-year-old. I think it's (reading) just something that we share that's a nice little calm time. It's a little connection … I think it's a lovely bonding time. You can sit and cosy up and it's quite intimate. Cuddly. Our time.

What became clear from the analysis of the data was that many of these parents enjoyed having an opportunity to spend quiet time with their children, which was valued and enjoyed. Being 'calm' and 'cosy' was associated with bonding as further expressed by Tara who reported that she sees a main purpose of reading being:

> To have family time – and it's nice to bond in that time because you can have a cuddle and cosy up and it's like a sharing point in time together.

However, not all parents seemed to think that shared reading needed to be calm and quiet to promote bonding. In fact, many parents spoke about using shared reading to create a loud and fun atmosphere, which was also highly enjoyable for both child and parent and also contributed towards bonding. For example, Bina spoke in detail about the fact that she and her husband tend to read in different ways, but both have the same 'end goal' – namely to make their daughter laugh. Similarly, Zainab described her shared reading interactions with her daughter as something that was animated and entertaining. When asked about the kind of things she does during shared reading she reported:

> Just like, you know, I make loud noises and stuff and say a word out of the book that's loud, not shouting, but loud. Or I say it really quietly and, you know, do things with my hands and stuff and just make her giggle and laugh.

What we are seeing here is that these parents are enjoying reading to their children, but the enjoyment is different for each individual. For some parents, shared reading is about creating a calm and relaxing atmosphere, where both parties can enjoy what Tania described as 'five minutes of shush'. For others, the enjoyment comes from creating a more raucous and entertaining environment, filled with laughter. This is not to suggest that parents will always read in the same way; it is of course perfectly possible for the same parent to enjoy reading in different ways to meet different priorities, though this was not something that the parents in this study specifically discussed. However, the project data did suggest that parents within the same family would often have different approaches to shared reading.

This was exemplified in Kylie's interview. Kylie told us that she herself was not confident with reading, but she did read regularly with her children which she 'loved'. She also told us that her husband often read to their young son, but tended to be far more animated in his approach than she is. This had made her question her own style of shared reading, to the point that she wondered if she 'bored' her son. However, she reported that she had come to the conclusion that 'it's just his dad reads differently' to the way she does. In the following extract, it is clear that Kylie has given careful thought to not only the different ways in which she and her husband read, but the affordances of these different reading styles for her son.

> His dad is a lot more into the voices and that ... and his dad goes 'raaaaaaaar'. But then when his dad reads to him, he doesn't settle – it makes him hyper. Also, if his dad's reading then he (the son) doesn't get into his book. He'll get more into the story in his head, so he'll be acting it out. Whereas when I read he'll sit and listen, so it's just two different ways of doing it really. He'll sit and look at the pictures with me, but with his dad the book is more in his imagination rather than looking at the words and the pictures.

Kylie is suggesting that the way she reads with her son has a different impact on her son in comparison with the reading her husband does. Firstly, Kylie is making the observation that her reading tends to have a settling effect on her son while her husband's reading tends to stimulate and excite. Clearly this can have practical implications for certain times of the day – for example, it stands to reason that many parents would prefer their children to be 'settled' rather than excited at bedtime! However, Kylie is suggesting that the different reading styles have a deeper impact on their son's engagement with the activity; she is claiming that her reading fosters an engagement with the book itself while her husband's reading encourages their son to develop his imagination.

Interestingly Kylie's comments were echoed by Sam, who, like Kylie, claimed that she was 'just not as good' as her partner in reading with her daughter. She reported, 'It's not as exciting when I do it. I probably will send her to sleep. It's boring.' However, Amy clearly enjoyed and valued the reading that both she and her partner shared with her daughter. This was especially salient given that Amy also reported that she did not enjoy reading for herself – a topic that is discussed in detail in Chapter 8.

Together this data illustrates the multifaceted character of parents' enjoyment of shared reading. The enjoyment may come from spending time with the child in a calm and relaxed manner, or it could involve something more lively and animated. Whatever the case, most parents in the study seemed to agree that the enjoyment of shared reading was associated with spending time with their child and bonding. What is more, some parents were clear about the fact that they knew they had to enjoy the activity if they were to be able to maintain shared reading practices. For example, Latika spoke of finding it hard to do much with her daughter because she was so busy with work and domestic duties. In addition, she also stated that she did not enjoy reading for herself, reporting that when she was a teenager she had tried to read novels but found it 'so boring'. However, Latika spoke enthusiastically about the fact that as an adult she enjoyed reading with her daughter, stating clearly that she reads because 'I enjoy reading for her – it's not that I'm forced'. Latika went on to explain that her enjoyment of the activity was crucial to the maintenance of shared reading when she reported:

> Yes I don't do anything that I don't like – I will do things that I like to do for her. If I don't want to do something I'll just tell my husband 'can you do this for her?'. If I'm not going to enjoy it, then I'm not giving 100 per cent what she wants, and she's not going to enjoy it with me, so what's the point.

What we are starting to see here is that parents' enjoyment of shared reading is complex. It is not sufficient to simply say that parents read with their children because they enjoy it, as this enjoyment is often directly related to the response that parents receive from their children. To return to Sam's interview, when asked how she felt about reading with her daughter she responded, 'I love it. If she laughs, I'm laughing.' This illustrates an important finding from the project with regard to parental enjoyment – these parents generally reported that gaining positive feedback from their child was an important aspect of the shared reading experience. Given that this has important implications for families who may need support in reading with their children, this suggests a need to look more closely at the relationship between enjoyment and feedback in order to understand parents' motivation for beginning or sustaining shared reading activity.

Links between enjoyment and feedback

The project data clearly showed that a key factor in parental enjoyment of shared reading activity was parents receiving feedback from their children, which indicated that the children were benefitting from the experience. The feedback that parents reported that they gained from their children included: evidence of learning, confirmation of the child understanding the book or story or signs of their enjoyment. Very often these factors were combined. For example, this was exemplified in Jo's interview. When asked how she felt about reading with her youngest child, Jo stated:

> I think at this stage, because she likes them (books), then I can (enjoy it). I wouldn't do it if she didn't like it, because I couldn't be bothered. But she's so engaged with books she does like, you know, counting, like the bits of toast there, or whatever it is.

In many ways Jo's comments mirror those of Latika, introduced in the section above. Latika went on to make the link between her child's enjoyment of the activity and her (Latika's) commitment to shared reading when she stated, 'She likes listening to the story, if she didn't like listening to the story I won't read to her.' What is clear is that both Latika and Jo are saying that certain conditions must be met if they are to read with their children. In Jo's case she is saying that her daughter is not only enjoying the activity, but is 'so engaged', manifest in the fact that she is counting, which was encouraged by the book they were sharing. Crucially, it is the *evidence* of this engagement that is impelling Jo to maintain shared reading activity with her daughter.

For many of the parents in this study, their enjoyment of shared reading was strongly linked to their child's enjoyment. This became a very familiar theme in the data and was evident within most of the interviews, in one way or another. For example, when asked about her views on the importance of shared reading, Hadra replied that she and her husband do it 'because she (daughter) enjoys it and it's something we can do together' and that importance, in terms of learning to read, 'doesn't come into it'. Katie also reported that her son 'loves' being read to and 'really enjoys it', while Kerry stated that her daughter 'enjoys it' and it makes her (Kerry) 'feel nice to know that she likes sitting listening to me reading'.

These parents were telling us that they valued getting feedback from their children to show that they (the children) were enjoying shared reading; as demonstrated, in some cases parents were quite clear that if they perceived this feedback to be missing, they would be less inclined to continue reading to their child. We will shortly discuss the different ways in which feedback was presented to, and interpreted by the parents, but before we come to this, it is important to examine this concept of child enjoyment in feedback in more detail. As already discussed, many of these parents seemed to believe that enjoyment was a distinct aim of shared reading; however, much of the data also suggested that for many parents, child enjoyment was also linked to the concepts of 'learning' and 'understanding'.

This was emphasised in several of the interviews, with Tania's being one such case. Tania spoke with enthusiasm about the pleasure that both she and her son derived from shared reading. There was no doubt that Tania saw mutual enjoyment as being a critical outcome of the activity, talking specific-ally about 'bonding' and 'quality time' as features of their shared reading. For example, Tania reported that, aside from bonding, her son 'gets enjoyment' out of shared reading, meaning that she would 'happily sit, if he wanted to carry on reading, for half an hour, which might mean that bedtime's done later'. What is more, Tania went on to make instinctive connections between this enjoyment, the feedback she was getting from her son, and the learning that was also taking place. Talking of being physically close when reading, Tania explained:

> It's always been like a bonding thing for us. And yeah – what he gets out of it. I can SEE him literally ... I mean you can see him taking it in. We both gain from it, definitely, it a good quality time.

What is clear from Tania's interview is that the enjoyment for her is embedded in the fact that she can see that her son is 'taking it in'. Tania provides further clarification on this when she later reported:

> The more questions he asks, the more ... you know ... he wants to learn, he really does, and I just ... he's so receptive I'll sit there all day, d'you know what I mean? If he wants to talk about blurbs on every book in the house I'd go through them with him.

Interestingly, while Tania's data supports previous research, which claims that bonding and enjoyment are key goals of shared reading for parents (Audet et al, 2008), we can see that for Tania, these factors are strongly linked with Tania's pleasure in seeing that her son is not only enjoying the activity, but is also learning from it. Further evidence to support this could be found towards the end of the interview when Tania again spoke about shared reading being 'good quality bonding time', before also saying 'and it's all going towards his future isn't it?'

Like Tania, Lisa also spoke about the relationship between enjoyment, feedback and learning in shared reading activity; however, she talked about her child's learning almost as a welcome consequence of the activity, rather than an actual aim. When first asked why she engaged in shared reading, Lisa's response was initially hesitant. She told us, 'I don't know. I just thought to start reading to them. I don't know. I think it's good to read isn't it?' Following on from this, Lisa then made the point that she reads because her daughter 'is enjoying it' before continuing with 'and I'm enjoying it as well'. As evident in many of the other interviews, when asked what it was about reading with her daughter that she enjoyed, Lisa responded, 'Mainly because I know she enjoys it, do you know what I mean? That's why I like reading with her'. This again shows that Lisa, like many other parents in this study, enjoyed reading to her child because she was getting positive feedback from the child in the form of seeing that her child was enjoying the activity; however, she was also making a natural connection between this and her child's learning. This is evident in the following extract from her interview. Having talked about her child's enjoyment, Lisa immediately stated:

> And I think it's just made her talk quicker, you know, things like her communication skills and stuff. Yes I think it's very important to read, and carry on reading ... So I'll carry on reading with her until she asks me not to.... So it's just seeing her enjoying it, and seeing how much her talking and her writing and things like that is coming on. Do you know what I mean – I think that's all down to reading.

Careful analysis of this data suggests that both Tania and Lisa value the learning that they can see taking place, and this contributed towards their enjoyment of shared reading activity; however, in both cases it appeared to be unlikely that either of these parents read to their children with the express purpose of promoting their child's learning. Rather, the main goals were to enjoy spending time with their child and to enjoy bonding; however, when the parents saw that the activity was also promoting learning, they felt even more committed to sustaining shared reading.

Interestingly, this emphasis differed from some of the parents in the study who were within a higher income bracket, who also spoke about the importance of their children enjoying shared reading; however, they also spoke specifically about the association between shared reading and their children's learning. For example, when asked about the reasons why she read to her son, Elizabeth responded:

At the beginning it was kind of … showing him pictures and teaching him things, like, pictures of balls. I suppose it's a teaching aid, but the first and foremost is just to enjoy the stories, it's an enjoyable thing to do with him. But then, yeah, it's been, I suppose, a kind of a teaching thing as well. He'll see something in a book and then he'll see it in the real world and he'll make the connection … When he was younger it was like teaching him the words for things, so it's a language thing as well. But, yeah, mainly it's just enjoyable to sit and have a cuddle and read a story, it's a quite nice bonding time with him.

While Elizabeth appears to agree that the enjoyment of reading should be the 'first and foremost' aim of shared reading, it is interesting to note that she is also talking about shared reading as an opportunity for not only 'learning', but for 'teaching'. In other words, Elizabeth is arguing that she can use the opportunity created by shared reading, to teach her son in various ways. This was further evidenced a little later in the interview when she again stated that shared reading should be 'enjoyable' but went on to say that it is important 'for his language and stuff'. She continued:

I think at this age it's really important that he starts to learn to read and write and speak and he's starting to express an interest in actually learning to read, so he'll look at the pages and say 'I don't know the words', and I'll say 'well we'll learn the words, we'll start learning them', and we've started doing like letters with him, and a bit of writing and a bit of reading.

Similarly, both Hannah and Victoria commented on the fact that shared reading offered an opportunity for their child to learn. When asked what drove her to initially start looking at books with her son, Hannah spoke in detail about societal expectations and her own perceptions of the importance of reading. She reported:

I think there was probably an expectation that that's what you do with children, so, we went to the library and they have Baby Time sessions don't they, where they read to them and sing a few songs, that kind of thing. And, you know, I recognise the importance of reading in terms of inspiring minds and opening up doorways to people as they get older.

Victoria also spoke about the 'importance' of reading in terms of a child's learning; however, she also emphasised that she wants her son to have a 'love of reading'. When asked what she wants her son to get out of shared reading activity, Victoria responded that it is about having nice 'family time' and that 'it's nice to bond in that time and have a cuddle'. However, Victoria had also bought phonics flashcards to use with her son, though she was quick to point out that she is 'not pushing the sounds', and does not want him 'to be bored'. That said, like Hannah and Elizabeth, Victoria was clearly aware that shared reading could support language development, which was something she was keen to encourage. She told us:

> I think it sort of helps with concentration and listening skills, and I know how important it is for vocabulary, and I know how important that is for young children, because if they've got the vocabulary they can express themselves. I know he's quite a shy child, so it's quite hard to express yourself in a social situation, like at school, nursery, so if he has got the words, that will help him. I also think it's (shared reading) a really good learning tool, a learning opportunity to find out about something new.

In pulling this together we can see that parents' enjoyment of shared reading is embedded in a cycle of reciprocity between parent and child. Many of the parents in this study were clear about the fact that their enjoyment was strongly dependent on their child providing feedback to show that they were getting something from the activity, such as enjoying it. This suggests that shared reading is a highly reciprocal activity, where both child and parent are not only jointly focused on a text but must be sharing a sense of enjoyment which is transmitted to one another. What is more, while enjoyment of shared reading remained a central concern for most of the parents in this study the data also indicated that this was linked to conceptualisations of child learning. While it was not the original intention of this study to compare the participants with one another, it became clear from the analysis that there was a difference in how some of the families from lower-income groups perceived child learning within shared reading, in comparison with some families who were in a higher income bracket. Most families across the whole data set reported that child enjoyment should be a key aim of shared reading activity; however, families from within lower income brackets were more inclined to report that they needed to see evidence of their child's enjoyment in order to maintain shared reading activity. What is more, some of these families went on to state that while the goal of shared reading was enjoyment, they were also aware that the activity was simultaneously promoting an aspect of their child's learning. Seeing evidence of this learning further encouraged the parents to enjoy shared reading with their child, therefore strengthening the cycle of reciprocity.

In contrast, parents from within a higher income bracket also stated that child enjoyment should be a main goal of shared reading; however, some of these parents also said that a goal of shared reading was to promote learning – especially language development. This is important because this suggests that these parents may be less dependent on gaining positive feed-back from their children given that they were also motivated to read to their children because it would support their child's learning. In fact, when asked directly if they would still maintain shared reading even if their children were not responding as positively as they were, Victoria reported that she 'would do it, but probably not as much', while Elizabeth also said that she would carry on reading and 'hopefully it'll sink in'.

This suggests that while receiving positive feedback from their children was clearly important for all parents, this may be especially important for some families within lower income groups. This, however, raises questions about what positive feedback looks like. How do parents interpret the feed-back they are receiving from their children and how does this impact upon their motivation to maintain shared reading activity with their children? This is discussed next.

Interpreting child feedback and the motivation to read

Feedback from children occurred in a variety of different forms, but a type of feedback commonly reported by parents related to embodied responses such as the child pointing to the text or smiling. It appeared to be the case that parents were particularly aware of their child's facial expressions during shared reading and used this to make judgements about their engagement. For example, Bina told us that she had previously struggled to find books that she felt her daughter seemed to like and had got to the point where she felt 'it's not working', when she had a 'breakthrough' by introducing her daughter to the book *Where's Spot?*. Bina reported that she was now getting the feedback she needed from her daughter when she stated:

> Now I'm happy to get her books because I can see that there's some-thing going on, like on her face – she gets it – she enjoys it. I'm not one of those to just do it and think 'hopefully it's going in'.

Very similar sentiments were expressed by Javid. Speaking of reading with his youngest son, Javid also spoke about his personal need to gain positive feed-back from his son's facial expression when he reported, 'He does listen and then I see his facial expression, that he's realised, he's understanding it kind of thing'. Javid went on to clarify that he (Javid) took this to mean that his son was 'getting it' and 'understanding what you're talking about' as well as 'enjoying it'. This also connects with Tania's comments, presented above, who also spoke about 'literally' being able to 'see' her son 'taking it in', which again demonstrates how parents were reading their children's facial expressions in order to gain the feedback they needed to maintain shared reading activity.

Other embodied responses which provided important feedback cues for parents included the child pointing at the book. For example, having stated that it was 'nice' to read with her son, Sarah (Dalton cohort; lives with her 2-year-old son and her teenage daughter; Sarah also has two older children who do not live at home) reported that this was because her son is 'listening and pointing to pictures' while she is reading. Lisa also told us that while she is reading, her daughter usually 'just sits and listens, or is pointing at the pictures and telling me what is going on', while Kerry stated that she knows that her daughter is happy to look at books because 'she will point to things and she'll tell me what is happening'.

Other parents in the study spoke about gaining verbal feedback from their child, such as their child asking questions or repeating parts of the text. In some cases parents talked about their children asking numerous questions during the shared reading; for example, Katie reported that her son 'does ask a lot of questions about things', before going on to give many examples of the kind of questions he may ask about the text. Similarly, Cathy explained how her daughter not only asked lots of questions during shared reading, but that this is only part of her engagement with the activity. She reported:

> We read a book, or she'll create a story, or I'll read and she'll be asking a mountain of questions or everything. Sometimes we don't read the story, we just have to look at the pictures and see what's on the page kind of, so there's a lot of aspects to it.

Cathy's data demonstrates how her child's questions are an essential element within the shared reading experience and influences the direction that the reading takes. This again shows how an aspect of child feedback, such as the child's questions, can have an impact on the parent and shape the way that the reading continues. This was also seen in Tania's interview when she said that 'the more questions he (her son) asks, the more I … d'you know what I mean, he wants to learn, he really does, and I just … he's so receptive I'll sit there all day'.

However, some parents reported that they were also aware that child responses, such as asking questions, were dependent on day-to-day circumstances and as a result they did not always expect their child to ask questions. For example, when asked if her son ever asked questions during shared reading activity, Hannah gave a detailed account of her son asking questions about a Peppa Pig book. She told us:

> Yes we were reading Peppa Pig the other day and he said, 'Why aren't they all eating pumpkin pie?', and I don't think I've read that one to him before, or haven't for a while because I thought 'I don't know, why aren't they?' And then a few pages later they were all

eating pumpkin pie, so I suppose he was asking questions about the order of the text.

Clearly there are times when Hannah's son does ask questions and responds verbally to a book; however, Hannah went on to point out that there are specific times when he would be unlikely to do this, but she would still regard him as engaged with activity. She reported:

> I think, probably, daytime reading I tend to link with him being tired or a bit unwell, so it might be that he's not quite so inspired then to ask questions. He's quite happy just snuggling and reading.

In this case, Hannah was suggesting that there were occasions when a lack of feedback from her child was not only accepted but was also expected. This was echoed in Hadra's interview when she reported that if it was getting late in the evening, then she would be less likely to pause the reading to invite questions and other verbal feedback from her daughter. In both these cases, a lack of verbal feedback from the child was unlikely to be interpreted negatively by the parents.

Together this suggests that the ways in which parents interpret feedback from their children may be highly individual and may also depend on factors such as the relationship between child and parent, or the specific circumstances of the day. Moreover, the particular feedback that parents are looking for may well depend on the parents' own specific goals for the activity. As discussed in the earlier part of this chapter, the project data indicated that while most parents wanted their children to enjoy shared reading, the essence of this enjoyment varied hugely. Sometimes parents wanted to engage in shared reading to promote a calming and relaxing environment – other times they wanted to create a fun and energetic atmosphere. This suggests that the ways in which parents interpret their children's responses may be dependent on the parents' own goals for the specific shared reading event. To illustrate, Natalie stated that she had had the instinct to read with her children at night, since they were babies. She told us:

> I always did that of a night. I don't know why.... It's nice – sends them to sleep. My babies always lay on me, so I'd be on the couch with a book and it's nice for them to hear your voice as they're going to sleep. Just chilling out with them.

Clearly in Natalie's case, she was reading with the intention of calming and settling her infants, so the fact that they fell asleep while she was reading was interpreted as positive feedback. This again demonstrates that shared reading is a highly individual activity, and that parents may want different things from the event. However, this is not in any way to suggest that parents are always leading shared reading. To the contrary, the project data strongly indicated that much of the shared reading that took place in these homes was in fact led by the children. This raises important questions about parental aims and motivations for reading as now discussed.

Child-driven reading and parental motivation

This chapter has so far demonstrated that the child's response to the activity was a critical factor in parents' motivation to maintain shared reading. Many parents in this study reported that they needed to see that their child was getting something from the activity, be it enjoyment, learning or a combination of the two, in order for shared reading to be sustained. This highlighted the importance of parents' receiving positive feedback from their child. One particular way in which the children in this study demonstrated their engagement with reading was evident in the fact that they often led the activity. To put this another way, parents in this study told us that they often read with their child because their child was asking to read, but this is not to suggest that shared reading took place because parents were simply 'obliging' their children. Rather these parents appeared to be motivated to read with their children *because* their children wanted to read, evident in the fact that they were leading the activity.

The project data provided numerous examples of parents telling us that their children often controlled *if* shared reading would take place, as well as *what, when* and *how* they read. To illustrate, having reported that her daughter had started to want to look at books by herself, rather than be read to, Bina had come to the conclusion that even though she (Bina) enjoyed reading with her daughter, she would allow her daughter to decide how reading would take place. She told us, 'Whenever she gets her books out it's, it's up to her, like, if she wants me, or if she wants to just look through it or whatever.' Bina enjoyed reading to her daughter and was happy to continue shared reading; however, having become aware that her daughter was starting to enjoy looking at books for herself, Bina allowed her daughter to decide whether the reading would be 'shared' or not. On a similar note, Fiona also told us that her son led much of the shared reading when she stated that her son 'definitely drives' a lot of the reading that takes place, explaining that 'he's the one that pushes the routine as much as anyone else'. Fiona went on to say that 'you couldn't say to him, 'Right we're not having books today.' He would refuse to go to bed!'

In both these cases it was clear that the parents were led by their children regarding whether shared reading would take place or not. Bina is talking about being invited into the activity by her daughter, while Fiona talked about her son 'pushing' the routine. But what does this mean for the parents' motivation to read? This was specifically addressed in Fiona's interview when she was asked if she would still read with her son if she did not have such a positive response from him. To this she replied, 'I don't know, probably not, well, certainly not as much.' This suggests that child-led reading may be motivating for parents and encourage them to maintain shared reading practices in the home.

The data indicated that parents in this study were also led by their children in terms of when reading took place. For example, when talking about when they read together Javid responded that it happens 'as and when they (his children) ask' and it 'just depends when he wants to and what his mood is'. Similarly, when asked if they have set times of the day when they read, Elaine (Barnwell cohort: lives with her 3-year-old daughter, three older children (one of primary school age and two who are at secondary school) and newborn twins) replied, 'no, just as and when she (her daughter) wants'. But this did not mean that parents always found it easy to read with their children when they asked to be read to. This was evident in Katie's comments when she reported:

> He does bring a book sometimes in the most awkward times like when you're doing the dishes or something. I just say 'let me finish doing the dishes and then we'll read your stories', he's like 'Can we do it now?', and I'm like 'Just give me a little minute and we'll get the dishes done and I'll sit and read your stories'. It sometimes can be a bit difficult, but I just try and get as much in as we can for him.

As discussed in the previous chapter, this shows how some parents allowed their children to direct when reading took place, regardless of whether or not they themselves orchestrated an actual routine for reading in the home. Similarly, the data also indicated that children would often decide *what* was read as well as *how* it was read. When asked to talk about the books that they read together Hadra spoke about the number of books they read each night, stating:

> One book. No, actually, having said that, sorry, she went through a period of at least five or six months where she had to read two books, and we read two books, and she's suddenly switched back to one. Even now, there are times she wants to read two ... we kind of follow her lead.

This was echoed in a number of interviews, with Kerry, for example, saying that her daughter goes to her dad and just gives him a book to share and then 'he'll sit and read'. Javid also provided a very detailed account of the way in which his son leads their reading, both in terms of what they read and how they read when he told us:

Their prompt was to come and sit with you and offer you (a book) ... They started it, you know like they got the ball rolling saying 'Oh, can you read this to me?' and not like the other way round.

Javid then went on to describe how his son directed the reading, firstly by choosing books about vehicles, a particular current interest, and also in directing how he wanted his father to read the book. The following extract gives a comprehensive and illuminating picture of their shared reading events. Javid reported:

He opened the book and he told me 'this paragraph, can you read that'. And if he gets another page and he recognises the picture or the story he ignores it and then he jumps to the next one, telling me to read that for him ... And I'm trying to read it all from start to finish, but he kind of looks at it and he boycotts that and skips it, and then points at another one and he goes 'read that one, read that one'.

The examples presented in this section clearly show how young children can have a major role in directing shared reading activity including *how* and *when* it happens as well as determining *if* shared reading occurs at all. This suggests that young children may exert considerable agency within the process, but it also demonstrates how valuable this can be in motivating parents to read or sustain shared reading activity with their children. This can perhaps be summed up in the words of Kylie who told us, 'When they want to read, you can't say no.' For many of the parents in this study, motivation to read with their children was dependent on their gaining feedback from their child to show that their child was enjoying the activity. Having a child initiate and/or direct shared reading was a powerful indicator for parents that their child enjoyed the activity. This in turn contributed towards parents' motivation for reading and encouraged parents to continue embedding it into everyday family life.

Conclusion

This chapter has shown how the parents in this study reported a variety of aims and motivations for reading with their children; however, most of them prioritised 'enjoyment' as a main goal of shared reading activity. But what this actually meant for parents was complex. The data clearly indicate that parents' own enjoyment of shared reading is embedded in a cycle of reciprocity between parent and child and is often directly related to the feedback that parents receive from their children. The responses parents receive from their children during shared reading activity can take a variety of different forms, and the extent to which parents perceive this feedback to be positive can depend on their aims for the activity. What is more, positive feedback from the children may provide parents with evidence of their child's engagement, enjoyment and/or learning, which in turn encourages parents to continue further reading events.

While the project data indicated that child feedback was important for most parents, it was clear from this study that families from within lower income brackets were more inclined to report that they needed to see evidence of their child's enjoyment in order to motivate them to maintain shared reading activity. This has major implications for families who may not read with their children (discussed in detail in Chapter 9) as it suggests that some parents may require particular support in handling what could be regarded negative, or limited feedback from their children. It further suggests that there is a need to explore and understand parents' own goals for shared reading with their children, within the context of intervention, as this too may have an impact on how they interpret and respond to the feedback they receive from their children. Following on from this, the next chapter looks specifically at some of the barriers that parents may face in reading with their children, including the impact of receiving negative or limited feedback from their children.

7

BARRIERS TO SHARED READING

Introduction

If we are to encourage and support parents in reading with their children, there is a need to understand potential barriers to shared reading activity in homes. As discussed in Chapter 3, previous research has attempted to identify barriers to shared reading activity in homes and this has identified that parent-centred factors such as parents being too busy with domestic or paid work commitments can prevent parents from reading with their children (Harris et al., 2007). In addition, child-centred factors, such as children appearing disinterested in the activity, have also been seen to impede shared reading (Bergin, 2001), as have structural factors, such as a lack of access to reading materials (Harris et al, 2007).

As we pointed out in Chapter 3, these studies have been helpful in identifying specific barriers to shared reading; however, the research design of these studies restricted parents to selecting barriers from a list of pre-existing factors rather than providing opportunities for parents to discuss how shared reading features in their everyday lives. Yet, as we have now demonstrated in detail in this book, understanding home literacy practices is a complex phenomenon and demands in-depth qualitative research that takes time to understand family lives and the ways in which literacy practices operate within.

Analysis of data from the Shared Reading Project partially supports previous research findings regarding barriers to shared reading, in that the reported barriers to shared reading were identified as being parent-centred or child-centred (Lin et al., 2015), though there was less emphasis on structural factors such as reading resources. While it was clear that the families in this study had different banks of reading materials, and accessed books in different ways, none of the parents spoke about having a lack of access to reading material. For example, several of the parents spoke about buying books for their children from bookstores, while others told us they often bought books in the supermarket. The library was used by some families, while others reported that they felt uncomfortable in using a library as they worried that their children would damage the books or be disruptive in the library. However, all parents spoke positively about the books that they read with their children, regardless of the amount of books they used or the content of the books and did not suggest that access to reading material was a barrier for them.

The project data revealed that barriers to shared reading could be identified as parent-centred (including factors such as the pressures of family life) and child-centred (including factors such as child feedback); however, the data also suggested that they could originate from outside of the actual family unit, therefore being described as cultural factors. What is more, the study also showed that these factors do not operate in isolation from one another but can work together to make shared reading activity harder, or more unlikely to happen for some families. As the Shared Reading Project allowed an insight into the complexities behind these factors, which were embedded in the everydayness of family life, this chapter therefore shows *how* certain barriers to shared reading can develop within homes, leading to the prevention of, or obstruction to shared reading activity.

The previous chapter highlighted that for many parents in the Shared Reading Project, certain conditions needed to be met if they were to begin or sustain shared reading with their children. In particular it was clear that many parents needed to see evidence that their children were getting something from the activity, meaning that the children were showing signs of enjoyment, understanding or both. This raises important questions about the ways in which negative feedback, or an absence of feedback from children can serve as a barrier to shared reading activity. This is discussed in detail later in this chapter. Before we do this, we firstly turn to look at the ways in which aspects of everyday family life can act as a barrier to shared reading.

Family life

While most of the parents in the Shared Reading Project did appear to read with their children, the data suggested that this was not always easy to implement. Some parents reported that competing demands on their time and energy, resulting from pressures occurring both inside and outside the home, had the effect of reducing shared reading activity with their children. For example, Kylie spoke in detail about the impact of moving house on their shared reading activity with their 3-year-old son. Having reported that they 'used to read every night', Kylie went on to explain how it became harder to maintain this since they moved to a new house. She reported:

> We moved here 5 months ago, and since we've moved in, we started off bedtime reading of a night, but we've slacked off because it's reading a book, and he's (her son) saying 'Again, again, again!' and you end up – it sounds terrible – but you're sitting there thinking 'you should be asleep by now'.

Kylie is suggesting that since moving to a new house, life has become more tiring and while she continues to value shared reading, it can cost time and energy. To demonstrate this point further, Kylie also spoke about the fact that she was able to read more frequently to her son before he was in Nursery and before she was working. She stated:

> We do still read but just not as often as what we used to. We used to sit every day. The only time he'd go to sleep was after his book – and then just during the day because he wasn't in nursery and I wasn't in work, we'd tend to read about three books a day … and he never used to go to sleep unless he had a story whereas now it's not like that.

Kylie is making the point that factors such as her work commitments make it harder for shared reading to happen, due to the fact that she now has less time to sit and read with her son. Not surprisingly other parents also spoke about everyday commitments, such as paid work, being factors that could obstruct shared reading. When asked about everyday activities in the home Latika began by saying 'I don't do much with her to be honest', before going on to tell us that this is because:

> Not only do I have to rush – do all my cooking, cleaning and every-thing, because I have to go to work after that. So I just do a little bit – like if she (her daughter) asks me 'let's do some play' – I don't know, like a pretend tea party or something.

While Kylie and Latika are both suggesting that the busyness of life can make it harder to read with their children, Javid also spoke about work inside and outside of the home being a factor that could make it hard to find time for shared reading. For example, when asked about the extent to which shared reading fits into everyday life Javid told us that 'it's not every day' that they read, but he was happy with the balance of time at work and at home as this made it easier to fit in activities such as shared reading. This was evidenced in his words:

> It (shared reading) fits in. Thankfully, you know, work is not full time, not too many hours – mine is barely more than 15 hours a week, and my wife's isn't much either – about 10 hours. So yeah – thankfully with all of the chores and routines we can fit it in.

One specific issue that a number of parents across the sample mentioned was that they found it hard to find time to read with their children indi-vidually when they had multiple children. In order to deal with this, several participants told us they would often share the evening routine with their partners, so it was quite common for parents to report that they would read with one child while their partner would read with another. Others reported that they would read to their children at the same time, which often meant that they would have to juggle between different books so that each child would share a book that was age appropriate at some point. However, the parents in this study generally reported that they wanted to spend 'quality time' with each of their children, and particularly valued having time to read with their younger children on a one-to-one basis.

Together this data suggests that factors such as paid work, household chores and family life can impede shared reading activity. This, in itself, is not a surprise, but what is interesting to note is that these same parents generally spoke very positively about shared reading, as discussed in the previous chapter. For example, though Latika claimed that she didn't 'do much' with her daughter, she also told us that her daughter enjoys listening to stories and that books are read to her every day. While it is true to say that Latika also pointed out that her husband tends to do more with her daughter than she does, to the point that she joked, 'I think you should be doing this interview with my husband because he spends more time with her', Latika also reported that she has 'read so many stories to her (her daughter)' and had gained personally from doing so. This suggests that while it can be hard to find time for reading, Latika does want shared reading to happen because it is enjoyable for herself, her husband and her daughter. Similarly, Kylie also spoke very positively about the experience of reading with her son. This was discussed in detail in the previous chapter, where Kylie was reported to say, 'I love reading with him' and spoke at length about the ways in which reading can fit into everyday family activity.

What we are therefore learning from this data is that even when parents enjoy reading with their children, and see that their children are benefitting from the activity, the everyday pressures of family life can still make it hard for them to find time to read, especially when they have competing demands on their time. Given this understanding, this suggests that it can be particularly challenging for parents to read with their children when there are other barriers to the activity, such as poor enjoyment from child or parent, or little positive feedback from the child. This is discussed in detail later in this chapter.

While it is fair to say that almost all of the parents in the Shared Reading Project did speak positively about shared reading with their children, the data did shed light on the reasons why parents from particular groups may not read with their children. Given that Kelly et al. (2016) found in their study that low-income mothers who were single were very unlikely to include shared reading in their discussion of children's bedtime routines, data from the Shared Reading Project provides some explanation for this. Firstly, it was clear from the data that many of the parents in this study shared evening routines, including reading at bedtimes, which meant that one parent could read with a younger child while the other put the older child(ren) to bed. Similarly, a number of mothers reported that they would take responsibility for the child(ren) earlier in the day, but the father would do the bedtime reading. This underlines the fact that shared reading, especially at bedtime when everyone is tired, can be challenging for any parent, even when they really want to do it; however, if there are two parents in the home, then it becomes easier to share the responsibility. It is therefore not surprising that it is more challenging for single parents to include shared reading into their everyday practices. What is more, the data also strongly indicated that shared reading happened because parents enjoyed doing it – this enjoyment included seeing that their children were also enjoying the activity and getting something from it. However, if parents are struggling with life in general, and family life is stressful, it stands to reason that family activities may lack enjoyment. This was evidenced in one case in the Shared Reading Project as now explained.

Roshana is an Iranian woman in her mid-thirties and lives with her husband and two children – a girl aged 3 years 6 months and a younger son under 2 years. At the time of the interview, neither Roshana nor her husband were currently in employment. Roshana also reported that she experienced depression. It was clear from the outset of Roshana's interview that she found life very difficult and this had an impact on her capacity to read with her children. To illustrate, when asked if she ever looks at books with her children Roshana provided the following response:

> Yes when we're – well I could, but you know, all my housework, and being with them, I don't have any time. I don't have nobody and a childminder is very expensive – you know to pay for example during the day. You know if I put him, like three hours, it costs lots of money – very expensive. I can't manage. My family income is very little.

What was immediately apparent in Roshana's interview was that she was finding the demands of home, in the context of limited resources, very challenging. It was also clear that life with two small children was incredibly difficult for Roshana, who spoke with frankness about some of the difficulties she faced on a daily basis. She spoke about the children tearing her books or newspapers, and the fact that they even 'broke the TV'. While she did report that her daughter had come to enjoy having a story read to her, it was difficult to manage as the younger son disrupted the activity. She reported:

> He would take it (the book). And I give another book to him, like a small one and children's ones, and I even change the pages for him, but he want just – I want to read for my daughter. I bring another book, he wants another book. Very difficult reading.

Roshana then went on to explain that when her daughter was younger she would push books away when she tried to read with her, so she stopped trying to engage her in shared reading. However, Roshana went on to report that 'after she (her daughter) started nursery it was very good – she by herself bring the books'. This, Roshana reported, was accompanied by her daughter 'smiling and things' when she looked at books, which resulted in Roshana trying to 'teach her colours' in books. This data again emphasises the importance of positive child feedback for parents in maintaining shared reading, as already discussed in detail in Chapter 6; however, Roshana went on to report that it was very difficult for her to respond to her daughter's requests for being read to, as her son would not allow the activity to happen. She told us that her daughter will choose a book and say 'mummy read this book' but when she is doing this, her son will 'take it away'.

Data from the Shared Reading Project indicates that the stresses of everyday life such as household chores, paid work commitments, ill health and financial concerns can all have an impact on shared reading activity in the home. But what the data also suggests is that factors such as these are complicated, and the extent to which these factors act as a barrier to shared reading will depend very much on the individual family. So far in this book we have shown how shared reading was conceptualised by many of these families as an everyday practice; motivations for reading included the fact that it was often child led and was also enjoyable for parent and child. However, if parents are struggling to gain enjoyment from shared reading activity, for whatever reason, then it is understandable that the activity may not happen. For example, even though Roshana's daughter wanted to be read to, and Roshana wanted to read with her, she (Roshana) was finding it hard to do this when she had both children together, as the younger child was seen to be disrupting the activity.

This raises serious questions about the ways in which families can, or should, be supported by practitioners in their shared reading practices. For example, reading interventions that essentially try to encourage parents to spend time reading with their children, or encourage more dialogic reading, without taking time to understand the family's individual circumstances, would most likely be ineffective for parents like Roshana, given the complexities that she has described in her interview. The implications of this study for wider intervention are discussed in detail in Chapter 9, but for the moment it is suffice to say that a strong message emanating from the Shared Reading Project is that there is a need for intervention that recognises the importance of parental enjoyment in shared reading activity. What is more, this enjoyment can be obstructed by the stresses of everyday family life, so it is important to support parents in dealing with these issues.

Having discussed some of the ways in which aspects of everyday family life can act as a potential barrier to shared reading practice in the home, we now turn to examine some of the other factors that may inhibit or prevent shared reading from taking place. As stated already, most of the parents in this study stated that they read, with varying degrees of regularity, with their children. However, the data also shone light on some of the factors that could potentially inhibit or prevent other parents from reading with their children. One such factor related to the role of their own socio-cultural background as now discussed.

Socio-cultural background

Many of the parents in the Shared Reading Project spoke about their own experiences of being read to – or not – within the context of their own childhood. For some, they wanted to access the books that they had enjoyed reading when they were children, so they could share these with their own children. This suggested that for some parents, their enjoyment of reading and their enjoyment of shared reading began in their own childhood. This was important because the data suggested that this had a strong impact on the shared reading activity they then carried out with their own children. For example, Elizabeth told us that when she read certain books to her daughter it brought back 'strong memories' of being read those particular books during her own childhood. She went on to talk specifically about 'the Allan Ahlberg books, like *Peepo* and *Baby's Catalogue*', which she remembered reading with her own mum. Similarly, Fiona stated that her daughter's favourite book at the moment is *Funnybones,* which she also remembered enjoying as a child, which reminded her that she would like to read *The Jolly Postman* to her daughter because 'I remember enjoying that one – I don't even remember who read it to me but I definitely remember it!'

Hannah reported that in looking for books for her son she has come across books that she enjoyed as a child such as *Mrs Pepperpot,* 'the William Price books' and *Ant and Bee.* She told us:

> I used to love all those and you want your child to really like them. No amount of *Mrs Pepperpot* will make my son like reading *Mrs Pepperpot* – there's some random sort of 70's ones that parents appear with and you go 'Oh I used to love that book!'. But they're just not interested. It's fair enough – they find their own way don't they.

What is interesting to note here is that although Hannah enjoyed certain books when she was a child, much as she would like her son to also enjoy these books, she is also aware that these books may be somewhat dated and therefore lack appeal to children today. Hannah is therefore making the point that what she really wants is for her son to experience the *love* she used to have for certain books, even if he doesn't love the same books as she did. Together this suggests that parents may be motivated to read with their children because they themselves have positive memories of being read to, and enjoying books, when they were children themselves. However, this raises questions about the role of parents' own childhood experiences in their motivations and barriers to shared reading with their own children.

Having been asked about the reading that took place in their own childhood homes, the parents in this study reported huge variation in their own experiences of being read to. What is more, the reasons why their own parents did, or did not read with them when they were children were deeply embedded in socio-cultural discourses. To illustrate, Latika spoke in detail about her upbringing in India, where her parents' 'first priority was studies', to the extent that there was concern that other activities would detract from study. For example, Latika reported that having friends was never a priority for her parents, and if she and her siblings made friends they would be told to 'make friends who are good in their studies'. When it came to home reading, Latika reported that the only books that were read were 'syllabus books' or 'books from school', and that they did not have 'storybooks and stuff like that', saying 'we don't have all these things in India'. Latika told us that she tried to read novels when she was in secondary school, because her friends were reading them, but she did not read for long because she found them 'so boring'. Interestingly though, when she did start reading these books, she reported that her father was dismissive of them, telling her that they were 'not important' and she should be focusing her attention on her studies instead. This led Latika to conclude that her parents believed that 'reading books (for pleasure) is wrong', although she also stated that her parents' views had changed in recent years.

Latika actually went on to develop a very positive shared reading relationship with her own daughter – this is picked up again in more detail in the next chapter, which looks specifically at the ways in which parents' own relationships with reading impacted on their shared reading relationships with their children. In Latika's case, she went on to enjoy shared reading with her own daughter but was aware that this would have been unusual practice in her own home culture. For example, she reported that she wanted to get 'into the habit' of shared reading, because 'we didn't have that habit (in India) ... and I see everybody reading here'.

Bina also talked about the role of her home culture in relation to her shared reading practices with her daughter. Although brought up in the UK, Bina described her family as an Asian British household; she reported that her father spoke English and Kurdish, but her mother spoke mainly Kurdish. Like Latika, Bina and her husband both read regularly with their daughter and seemed to enjoy this, yet when asked if her parents had ever read to her, Bina responded 'No – we don't come from a culture that does anything like that'. However, Bina went on to report that her dad was 'really into education', and this meant that he was very happy to buy books for Bina and support her love of reading.

105

What we are seeing from this data is that activities such as shared reading are influenced by factors such as culture. This resonates strongly with the studies of Heath (1982) and Brooker (2002), discussed in detail in Chapter 3, which showed that activities such as bedtime stories are not 'natural' but are situated within specific discourses which are influenced by the culture of the family. However, like Brooker (2002) also pointed out, a child's home culture is not in any way a uniform construct but is 'a complex combination of family circumstances past and present' (57). This complexity was highly apparent in the Shared Reading Project data. Both Latika and Bina did not experience shared reading within their own childhoods, and both spoke about this being related to the culture within which they were situated. This suggests that broad cultural expectations may act as a barrier for some parents in reading with their children; if shared reading is not part of a family's cultural background then parents may not consider reading with their children. However, the data also indicates that this can combine with individual family cultures, meaning that the extent to which shared reading features within everyday family practices is unique to each family.

To illustrate, when Tara was asked if her parents read to her when she was a child her initial response was 'I can't remember them doing this', which was quickly followed by this account.

> They're not very up on education and stuff. They're hard workers, but anything educational – that's not really their strong point. So it was like 'you do what you're told – you work' ... Just go to work, do your job, pay your rent – that sort of thing.

Tara appears to be suggesting that activities such as shared reading did not feature within her own childhood, because this was quite simply not something that her parents would have done. From what Tara is saying, activities such as shared reading were seen to be part of an educational discourse that was detached from her parents' way of life, which was focused on working hard in order to meet the financial costs of daily living. Interestingly, Tara went on to report, later in the interview, that her dad read books himself and was 'always in the library', clarifying that he did not read fiction but did read 'a lot of biographies'. This shows that while reading did feature in Tara's childhood home environment, shared reading did not. This raises questions about the extent to which 'shared reading' is seen as 'reading', or whether it is conceptualised as something quite different to traditional constructions of reading. This is an important question and is considered in detail in the next chapter. For the moment though, what is clear is that parents of young children today may well have come from homes where shared reading was simply not part of everyday family life.

When asked about shared reading within their own childhood homes, some other parents in the study talked instead about other activities that they engaged with. For example, Cathy reported that she could not remember being read to as a child but did have strong memories of sitting on a step with her family 'with a duvet around us, watching a thunderstorm – those kind of things'. She went on to say that she enjoyed 'me and mum time' where they were 'always snuggled up with loads of cushions on the sofa, or quilts', so they could lay on the floor together and watch programmes like *Little House on the Prairie*. Similarly Mia (Barnwell cohort: lives with her husband and their two sons, the youngest of whom is 3 years and 5 months and the older who was of primary school age) also struggled to remember if she had been read to as a child, but she spoke of having strong memories of spending time together as family, especially when eating. She reported:

> I think there's some nice feelings, nice experiences you remember. For me personally – I know it's a simple thing – but eating around a table ... I always make a big deal of eating around the table because I remember that. I remember my dad coming home and we always ate around the table ... My dad would be 'right – tell me about your day', and we'd end up arguing (laughs) ... but I always remember being sat around the table.

What is interesting to note is that even though these parents cannot remember being read to as children, the question of shared reading triggered other memories of being close to their parents and enjoying time together. This is important because, as seen in previous chapters, factors such as enjoyment were critical in motivating many of the parents in this study to read with their children. Yet what we are learning from these parents' reflections of their own childhoods is that there are other family activities that can provide closeness and enjoyment other than shared reading – or possibly instead of shared reading. This may be especially likely if shared reading is not embedded in the culture of the family.

This raises two points. Firstly, this underlines the need for us to recognise that shared reading may not be part of the family discourse and/or family culture of the children and families with whom we are working. This is not in any way to suggest that these parents are not spending time with their children – they may well engage their children in a variety of activities that promote factors such as closeness and conversation. However, as raised in the introduction, it is important to remember that shared reading is particularly beneficial for young children. Having found that the talk occurring between parent and child during shared reading activity is often more complex than talk which happens during other activities (Fletcher & Reese, 2005), further research suggests that this may be linked to the fact that during shared reading activity, the text triggers a joint attention between parent and child that supports the development of language skill (Kucirkova et al., 2018; Karrass, Braungart-Rieker et al., 2002). This indicates a need for practitioners to understand how parents perceive shared reading and find ways to encourage parents to read with their children, based on their knowledge of the individual family culture and discourse.

Secondly, this data again highlights the fact that the role of enjoyment in shared reading activity cannot be overlooked. This chapter has shown that parents very often want to enjoy spending time with their children, which ties closely with findings reported in previous chapters which showed that enjoyment is a critical motivation for shared reading activity. This suggests that a lack of enjoyment, or a lack of child feedback to demonstrate enjoyment, could be a major barrier for some parents in reading with their children. This is discussed next.

Feedback and enjoyment

As highlighted in Chapter 6, gaining enjoyment from shared reading activity was a prime concern for most of the parents in this study. Parents' enjoyment of the activity was often closely associated with the feedback they received from their children, which provided them with evidence to show that their child was benefitting from the activity. This in turn motivated the parents to carry on reading with their children. This was clear in comments from several parents such as Jo who reported that she enjoys reading with her daughter because her daughter 'likes books', concluding that she 'wouldn't do it if she (her daughter) didn't like it, because I couldn't be bothered', however she does read because her daughter is 'so engaged with books'. Similarly, Latika also told us that her daughter 'likes listening to the story', before going on to emphasise that 'if she didn't like listening to the story I won't read to her'.

These parents were clearly stating that they simply would not read with their children if they were not getting the positive feedback from their child to show that the child was engaged and enjoying the activity. This strongly suggests that if some parents do not feel as if they are getting positive feedback from their child, they might be disinclined to initiate shared reading. This shows that there is a huge element of reciprocity in the shared reading relationship that parents may develop with their children as seen in Figure 7.1. However, if this cycle does not develop, or is broken, shared reading activity may not take place. What is more, the data from the Shared Reading Project suggested that while receiving positive feedback from their children was clearly important for all parents in the study, this may be especially important for some families within lower income groups as discussed in Chapter 6. This indicates that it may be especially important to support these families in developing strong reciprocal shared reading relationships with their children. The implications for practitioners who are supporting families in shared reading activity are discussed in Chapter 9.

108

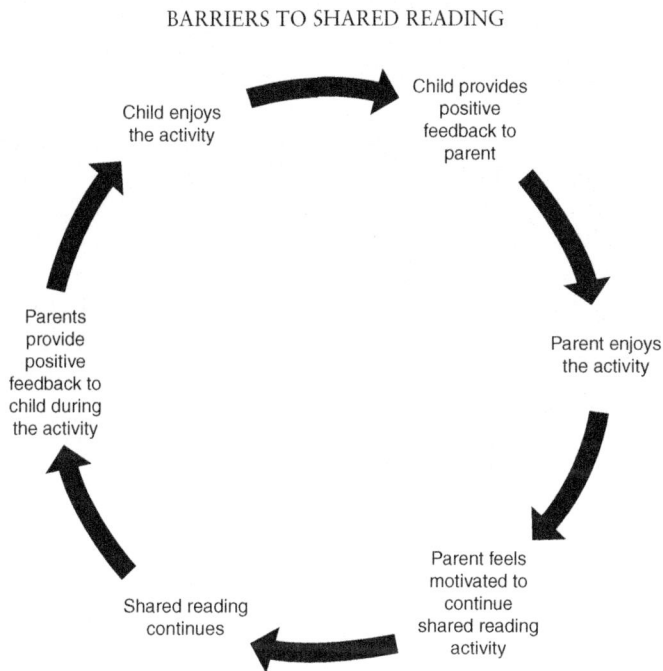

Figure 7.1 Cycle of reciprocity.

As highlighted in Figure 7.1, we can see that parental enjoyment is a critical factor in the maintenance of shared reading activity, and parental enjoyment is often strongly linked with the feedback parents receive from their children during the event. But this raises further questions about the ways in which parents may interpret the feedback they get from their children. Moreover, this may be a particular issue if the child is very young and therefore not yet able to give the kind of feedback that some parents appear to need if they are to maintain shared reading activity. The project data suggested that some of the parents in this study either did not read with their children when they were babies because they did not believe that the child was 'ready', evidenced by their behaviour, or having tried to read with their child, they stopped because they were not receiving what they perceived to be positive feedback from the child.

Over half the participants reported that they had started shared reading when their child was a baby, most commonly at six to eight months when their baby could sit independently. However, many of these parents spoke about challenges that had stopped regular shared reading. For example Sarah told us that she had tried to look at books with her son when he was under 2 years old, but stated that he had 'never been bothered about reading' and was 'not interested', concluding that 'there's no point, they don't understand . . . when they're babies'. Similarly, Bina had tried to look at books with her daughter as a baby, but reported that 'at the beginning you think "she's way too young … she doesn't get this"'.

In coming to the conclusion that their children were not ready to be read with, parents described 'negative' embodied responses such as the child crawling away, not sitting still or looking bored. For example, Sarah explained how during shared reading her son 'wouldn't settle … you know wanting to look at something else or get something else'. Similarly, Latika reported that her daughter would 'get distracted so easily … if I'm reading a book to her, and then she's not even interested'. Parents also spoke about other physical responses, such as their child cutting books and pushing books away (Roshana), reporting that they saw these as signs of a lack of enjoyment. The impact of this perceived negative feedback on the parent was particularly evident in Farah's interview, who reported that her daughter 'doesn't like books … when I want to read the books for her she's … trying to just pick … another page'. Farah went on to explain that she was trying to read the book from start to finish, but her daughter wanted to skip backwards and forwards in the text. Farah perceived this as evidence that her daughter did not like books, especially because she was not giving other feedback such as labelling or asking questions.

Together this indicates that some parents might be unlikely to read with their children when they are babies or toddlers, because the child does not give the feedback that parents need to initiate or maintain shared reading activity. However, this does not mean that the child *is* disengaged with the activity. As highlighted in their book about working with babies and toddlers from birth to three, Nutbrown and Page (2008) outline some of the research evidence demonstrating the capacities of babies which has shown that even the youngest babies can distinguish human faces and recognise a familiar face, and show preferences for certain objects and images (Gopnik et al., 1999), indicating that babies need interesting surroundings and stimulation. Further studies have contributed to our understanding of how babies and toddlers develop (Gammage, 2006; Meltzoff & Moore, 1999), suggesting that 'babies are born with innate tendencies of curiosity and recognition and that adults can confidently harness these natural tendencies in order to support those early skills (Nutbrown & Page, 2008).

This suggests that one of the roles of practitioners working with parents of children under the age of three, could be to support parents in handling feedback from their children during shared reading activity. There may be a need to encourage parents to recognise that child responses such as pushing a book away, grabbing books or getting distracted are not necessarily signs that a child is not ready for shared reading, or dislikes it, but might simply mean that the child needs something else at that moment in time. In other words, these actions from the child are not necessarily 'negative' but may be natural and normal responses for any young child in response to any activity. However given that the Shared Reading Project demonstrated that it could be difficult for parents of young children to maintain shared reading activity if they are not receiving positive feedback from their child, this indicates a need for parents to be supported in the way that they manage shared reading when they do not receive positive feedback from their children. This suggests that there is a need for practitioners to support parents in how they deal with an absence of feedback, or what parents perceive to be negative feedback. Specific strategies to support families with this are discussed in Chapter 9.

Conclusion

This chapter has shown that just as shared reading may happen for many different reasons, there are a number of factors that may inhibit or prevent the practice from taking place. What is more, this chapter has also shown that these factors may interweave with each other, making shared reading activity harder, or simply more unlikely to happen for some families.

The overwhelming finding from the Shared Reading Project showed that for many of the participants in this study, the shared reading encounter had to be enjoyable if parents were to maintain shared reading activity with their children. This suggests that if parents are not reading with their children, it is important to not just encourage them to read, but to support the family in finding ways to make the activity enjoyable for both parent and child. However, the data suggested that for some families the situation may be even more complex.

It was clear from the data that the everyday pressures of family life can be a barrier to shared reading activity. Parents spoke about factors such as lack of time, stress, financial concerns, moving to a new house, ill health and so on, as having an impact on their ability to read with their children, even when they were motivated to do so. Difficult family circumstances will always be a barrier and it is important for us to work with families to understand how factors such as financial worries, mental and physical health issues and so on can have an impact on the ways in which parents spend time with their children including engaging in shared reading. However, when we consider that shared reading appears to be dependent on both parent and child providing positive feedback to the other, in a cycle of reciprocity, this suggests that if, on top of the everyday pressures of family life, shared reading is not enjoyable, parents may be less inclined to initiate the activity. This has particular implications for families who are living with severe challenges in their lives. If these parents are also not getting positive feedback from their child when shared reading is attempted, then shared reading could become even more unlikely to happen.

The data further suggested that shared reading may not take place because it is not part of a family's cultural discourse. As raised in this chapter, these parents may well be engaging their children in a variety of activities that promote features such as closeness or talk, but shared reading may simply not feature as a family practice. This again has implications for practitioners working to support these families in reading with their children, indicating a need for practitioners to understand how parents perceive shared reading and find ways to support parents based on their knowledge of the individual family culture and discourse.

In summary, this chapter has demonstrated that barriers to shared reading, and the ways in which barriers to reading may develop, are highly complex. Just as shared reading practices are unique to the individual family, the reasons why parents may not read with their children are also particular to the individual family. This again underlines the importance of practitioners taking time to understand the families with whom they are working, so that support can be appropriately directed. That said, there is a clear need for practitioners to help parents to gain enjoyment from reading with their child, as this appears to be critical to the maintenance of shared reading for many. But this raises further questions about the role of parental enjoyment in shared reading activity. What if parents do not enjoy reading for themselves – or have had a poor personal relationship with reading over the years? Could this have a negative impact on their shared reading practices with their own children? Or perhaps act as a barrier to shared reading taking place at all? The next chapter considers these questions by examining the relationship that the parents in this study had with reading themselves, and the extent to which this linked with shared reading practices with their own children.

8

PARENTS' RELATIONSHIPS WITH READING AND LINKS WITH SHARED READING PRACTICES

Introduction

Alongside asking parents in this project to talk about the reading they did with their children, we also asked them to talk about their own relationship with reading. This allowed us to analyse the relationship between these two components of the data and understand the link between the parents' own relationships with reading, and their shared reading practices with their children. One main reason for doing this was to investigate if having a seemingly poor personal relationship with reading, which might have included, for example, a dislike of being made to read aloud at school, could inhibit parents in reading aloud with their own children. The data from the Shared Reading Project clearly showed that this was not the case for the parents in this study. While about a third of the parents participating in this study reported that they did not enjoy reading for themselves, or had had what might be regarded as a 'poor' relationship with reading when they were a child, they all went on to develop strong shared reading relationships with their own children. The importance of this finding lies not only in the knowledge that parents who have, or have had poor relationships with reading themselves can, and do, go on to have enjoyable and productive shared reading relationships with their children, but in understanding the interplay between these relationships. This chapter therefore presents an insight into the ways in which parents' own reading relationships connected with their shared reading practices with their children, and the implications of this for work with other families in supporting shared reading in the home.

Understanding parents' own relationships with reading

As discussed in the previous section, several studies have explicitly explored the barriers to shared reading with young children (Harris et al., 2007; Lin et al., 2015); however, very little is known about the relationship between parents' own reading and their reading relationships with their children. In order to understand this, interviews in the Shared Reading Project devoted considerable time to talking to parents about their own reading, both as a child and as an adult. For example, parents were asked to talk about any shared reading activity that their own parents had conducted when they were children, and whether or not they had enjoyed reading when they were children. As a result, we developed five overarching themes from the data which were:

- Parent attitude to school/experiences of school
- Parent reading as a child (including being read to)
- Parents' reading as an adult
- Shared reading relationship with child
- How parent and child read together.

Analysing the data within these themes allowed us to understand the parent's own personal relationship with reading, as a child and as an adult, and situate this alongside the shared reading relationship that they had developed with their child. In order to do this, we had to firstly categorise the participants; we did this by developing the categories of participants who reported that they:

- *did* read as a child/ young adult and *does* read to own child now
- *did not* read as a child/ young adult and *does* read to own child now
- *did not* read as a child/ young adult and *does not* read to own child now
- *did* read as a child/ young adult and *does not* read to own child now.

These categories were informed by the work of Moss (2000) who developed three categories of readers in order to investigate the different ways in which boys and girls react to proficiency judgement within the context of the junior school reading curriculum. These categories were: 'those readers who *can and do* read freely; those who *can but don't* read freely; and those who *can't yet and don't* read freely' (2000: 102). To return to the Shared Reading Project, it should be noted that the purpose of using this categorisation was not to make a quantified statement about the amount of families that fell into each category, but to help us to focus on the data that allowed us to understand if parents who either had a poor relationship with reading themselves as a child and/or as an adult, were able to develop positive reading relationships with their own children. Of course the individual profiles of participants within each category varied substantially; for example, some participants in the '*did not* read as a child/ young adult and *does* read to own child now' group reported that they disliked reading at school and do not read as an adult, while others started to enjoy reading at a later stage in life. This again underlines the fact that while the categorisations alone did tell us something about the links between parents own relationship with reading and their shared reading relationships with their children, the depth of understanding came from analysing the data within the individual interviews.

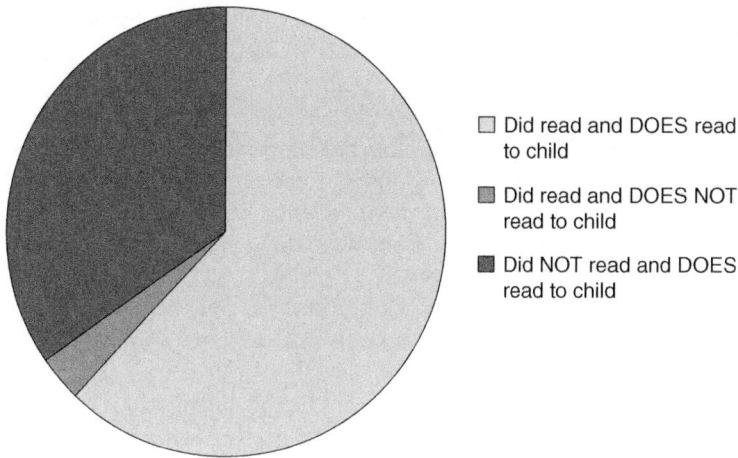

Figure 8.1 Link between parents' reading as a child/young adult and their shared reading relationship with their own child.

Having analysed the data according to the themes presented, we found that 18 out of the 29 parents could be categorised as '*did* read as a child/ young adult and *does* read to own child now'. Ten of the parents were assigned the category '*did not* read as a child/young adult and *does* read to own child now' while only one parent fell into the category '*did* read as a child/ young adult and *does not* read to own child now'. This parent (Roshanna – whose data was discussed in Chapter 7) spoke about wanting to read to her children, but felt unable to, due to factors such as health issues. No participant fitted the category '*did not* read as a child/young adult and DOES NOT read to own child now'. See Figure 8.1 for an illustration.

The data discussed in this chapter looks primarily at the parents in the category '*did not* read as a child/ young adult and *does* read to own child now', as this allowed us to understand the factors that motivated parents who did not enjoy reading for themselves, to read with their children. This has important implications for the ways in which educationalists can target the support of other parents who do not appear to have a strong relationship with reading themselves, in encouraging them to enjoy reading with their own children.

School and the development of poor relationships with reading

As this book has so far highlighted, enjoyment plays a crucial role in motivating parents to read with their children. The previous chapter showed how enjoyment features within a cycle of reciprocity within the shared reading relationship (see Figure 7.1 in Chapter 7) as both child and parent need to be enjoying the activity in order for it to be maintained by some families. When we turn our attention to parents' own relationships with reading, it became quickly apparent that most parents within the category '*did not* read as a child/ young adult and *does* read to own child now' spoke about the fact that they did not enjoy reading when they were at school. This raises some interesting questions about the reasons why these parents, who did not enjoy reading at school, came to enjoy reading with their own children. In particular, we are compelled to question what this says about the construct of *reading* within these two contexts?

It was not a surprise that when asked to talk about their own interactions with reading, many of the participants in this category spoke about school, stating that their experiences of reading at school were often negative. In particular, many of the comments were focussed on being made to read aloud in class, which was clearly stressful and intimidating for some. For example, Bina told us that while she was expected to read aloud during her secondary school education, she 'wasn't confident' and 'didn't like doing it', as the whole process made her feel 'shy'. The potential anxiety associated with the expectation to read aloud in class was almost always associated with a fear of not being able to read particular words in a book. This was also apparent in Fiona's interview, who spoke about 'English Literature' and the fact that 'the teacher would read some and then he'd pick people to read out of the book'. When asked how she felt about this Fiona reported:

> Yeah, I just remember that nervous feeling of, it went – oh no, when he comes to me to read, is there gonna be … you'd be trying to skim through to see if there are any big words that you might not be able to pronounce, that kind of thing. I remember that anxiety a little bit.

Similarly, Kylie directly connected the fact that she never read for pleasure, with being made to read aloud in class when she stated, 'I never read myself. I can remember reading out in class and I wasn't confident around them and I'm still not. I don't enjoy reading – not out loud'. Bina, Fiona and Kylie all articulated a feeling of stress and anxiety, which they associated with being made to read aloud in class, given that they were not confident in their ability to read aloud with fluency. Although not focussed on reading aloud specifically, Natalie also spoke about a fear of public humiliation in relation to not being able to read certain words in texts at school when she said:

> I've got certain memories in English where I couldn't read certain words and I used to have to ask the teacher and obviously you don't want to have to ask the teacher in front of kids. I can remember it was a big long word and I remember thinking, I didn't know what it was and I got the question wrong. I knew I'd got the question wrong

116

because I couldn't understand what the word was but I didn't want to ask the teacher.

What we are seeing here is that when asked to talk about their own relationship with reading, these parents were all reporting that school, in one way or another, made them feel self-conscious about their reading ability, which was on public display. In each of these cases the participant spoke of the requirement to 'pronounce' a word correctly or make sense of a word for the purpose of getting a question right. In other words, these parents were not only describing reading as a compulsory experience which was testing their ability to decode print, but were telling us that a failure to meet this requirement could result in public humiliation.

These parents were reporting that their own relationship with reading was damaged by the fact that perceived deficits in their own reading abilities had the potential to be exposed during lessons in school. This suggests that the potential judgement of 'others' was a significant factor in the development of a personal relationship with reading at school. Further data indicated that the perceptions and behaviours of other students was also important, particularly in relation to reading being seen as a mark of social acceptance. For example, when asked to talk about reading as a child, Bina stated:

> My experiences of reading were having a Tracy Beaker book 'cos I thought that was cool at the time, because my friends had them. That might have been beginning of secondary school, but I never actually read them.

Bina is stating that when she was at school she liked the idea of reading certain books because this was seen as a 'cool' thing to do; however, she did not enjoy reading the books and therefore did not manage to conform to this norm. This notion of wanting to read in order to meet a social norm was also expressed by Latika. When describing reading during her secondary school education Latika told us:

> I did do a little bit of, erm, start reading because my friends were reading, and I said 'ok, I'll start reading novels and stuff', because my friends are doing it, just … because they are doing it. But I found it so boring.

Both Bina and Latika are reporting that they tried reading novels when they were in secondary school because they believed they ought to be reading them, evidenced by the fact that their friends were reading certain books; however, they both struggled to meet this social norm because they did not enjoy reading. This was further demonstrated when Bina stated that even now she 'wouldn't choose to get a book and read'. She went on to say that she 'wished' she was 'like that' (being someone who enjoyed reading), but she has 'just never been like that'. Similarly, Latika spoke of other people who would say 'I love reading! I love reading', which made her think 'I'm the only one on this Earth who doesn't like reading'. These words were echoed by Kylie who also spoke about her lack of reading in relation to others when she reported, 'You know when people go on holiday and get into a book? I just can't get into one'. Kylie was able to trace her disengagement from reading back to her school days when she reported that she 'never read', 'wasn't confident' and did 'not enjoy reading ... out loud'.

What we can see emerging from this data is that reading, for these participants, was not a comfortable activity during their school years. Their excerpts are describing reading as something of a challenge, connected with difficulty and/or a lack of confidence in their ability to decode print with accuracy. As a result, these participants were not confident in reading aloud during school lessons. This is not surprising given that situations such as this meant that their reading was very much on public display and therefore open to the judgement of others. Interestingly though, these participants not only spoke about these issues in relation to reading inside of the classroom, but also indicated that there was a social norm to read for pleasure outside of the classroom. Given that they did not enjoy reading books for pleasure, they could not participate in this social convention with their friends, even though this is something that they would have liked to do.

These participants are therefore reporting that they developed poor relationships with reading during their secondary school education. It would be unfair and indeed inaccurate to suggest that our data indicated that the school discourse was directly responsible for this – we cannot say why exactly this relationship with reading developed. But what we can see is that reading, as a construct, was fraught with expectations during this period in the participants' lives. These parents described a range of judgements that were attached to reading, which included judgements from teachers and peers on their ability to decode print with accuracy, read aloud with fluency and enjoy reading popular books. These participants were unable to meet these imposed expectations and therefore declared that they did not have a good relationship with reading. Yet despite this, these same participants went on to report that they had gone on to develop positive shared reading relationships with their own children when they became parents themselves. This has important implications for understanding how parents who may not have a strong personal relationship with reading can go on to enjoy reading with their children.

Developing positive shared reading relationships with their children

The above section has shown how for most of the participants in the '*did not* read as a child/ young adult and *does* read to own child now' category, their own reading was described as something of a struggle. Much of what they are reporting can be summed up in the words of Hadra who actually became an avid reader later in life but did not enjoy reading at school. Hadra told us: 'I used to struggle a lot in school with reading... I wasn't really into it I, I suppose, as in actually reading books, so, yeah, I used to struggle a lot'.

This concept of reading being a 'struggle' and something that they are not 'into' was very evident in these participants' accounts of their own reading; however, these sentiments did not exist within their descriptions of their shared reading experiences with their own children. In contrast, reading with their children was described as being easy, relaxed and enjoyable. For example, Kylie who told us that she herself 'never read', 'wasn't confident' and did 'not enjoy reading ... out loud' went on to describe reading to her son as being 'so easy'. She reported:

> I think it's one of the easiest things you can do, because you can sit and read for half an hour or five minutes, it's just something that you can fit in. There's no cleaning up afterwards. Just put the book back and get on. You can do it while the tea is getting cooked, things like that.

The notion of reading being 'easy' contrasted starkly with Kylie's reflections on her own reading when she was at school. Similarly Latika, who had told us that she had tried to read novels when she was in secondary school, but had found 'it so boring', went on to report that she reads with her daughter because she 'enjoys reading for her', going on to emphasise that this is the reason why she reads and 'it's not that I'm forced'. As discussed in Chapter 6, Latika was especially clear about the fact that she would only read with her daughter so long as they were both enjoying it. There was no indication that she found shared reading boring, in fact she even went as far as to say that she now believed that reading is a valuable activity for her daughter because 'if you're reading you just don't feel bored'.

Although these participants spoke about their own reading in relation to their children's, they clearly felt much more positively about the concept of reading within the context of shared reading with their children, in comparison with their own experiences of reading for themselves. What is more, in many cases they explicitly stated that they wanted their own children to enjoy reading. This was evident in Natalie's interview when, speaking of her older children, she reported:

> I want them to enjoy it and want to do it. So I try and get them to enjoy it. So I was a bit disappointed in the school when they said they were focusing more on phonics and things.

Having reported that one of the reasons why she did not enjoy reading when she was at school was because she felt embarrassed about her ability to decode print, and did not want others in the class to be made aware of her difficulties, it is interesting to note that Natalie was keen for her children's school to prioritise enjoyment over phonics instruction. In other words, having not enjoyed reading when she herself was at school, Natalie wants her own children to gain enjoyment from reading and remains concerned that certain approaches in school could intrude upon this.

What we are learning from this data is that even when parents report having, or having had, a poor relationship with reading themselves, they still can go on to have positive and enjoyable relationships with reading through the context of shared reading with their children. This is important given that we have already established that enjoyment is a vital factor in the maintaining shared reading activity. This suggests that for these parents, *reading* within the context of shared reading with their children has become a quite different construct to the reading they were struggling with when they were at school themselves. This is discussed next.

Shared reading; a different definition of 'reading'?

The parents in the Shared Reading Project who did not have a good personal relationship with reading spoke about reading as an activity that they did not enjoy. They also spoke about their secondary school years as being a time when their reading was on public display and was governed by expectations, both in terms of their ability to read with accuracy and the social expectation that they should be enjoying reading certain books. However, this stood in sharp contrast to the way in which they came to define *reading* within the context of their shared reading activity with their children. For many of these parents, shared reading was not only about reading a book together but was seen as a valuable opportunity for them to spend protected time with their child. This was evident in Natalie's interview when she spoke of shared reading as:

> It's our little bonding time really, that time together. It goes off books as well, just because we've got books in our hand, we talk about the rest of the day, we get a story in, but then that's our time.

Natalie is here articulating that her shared reading encounters with her children are about much more than reading the book. Having stated that the activity provides time for her to bond with her children, she goes on to explain that the parent–child interaction occurs *because* they have a book to share together but is not limited to reading the book. Just because they have 'books in (their) hand', their interaction is not restricted to just getting 'a story in', but includes talking together about their day, 'bonding' and gener-ally having 'time'. In other words, the book appears to be acting as a cata-lyst in facilitating the opportunity for parent and child to spend quality and protected time together, which includes talking and indeed bonding.

Very similar sentiments were expressed by Hadra. Interestingly, Hadra reported that it was her husband who tended to read to their daughter; how-ever, unlike Hadra, who became interested in reading at a later stage in life, she spoke of her husband as being someone who 'doesn't read at all'. When describing the shared reading interaction between her husband and daughter, Hadra emphasised the fact that the activity again extended beyond reading. She reported:

> So he gets her changed and reads her book, and then just tells her some stories and asks her about her day. So they talk – I wouldn't say rubbish (laughs), they talk randomly, and then he'll tell her a story, and I take her up to bed.

Not only is Hadra's husband another example of a parent who appeared not to have a good personal relationship with reading, but had developed a strong shared reading relationship with his child, but this again illustrates how reading, within a shared reading context, includes time for talking and for parent and child to enjoy one another's company. This clearly differs from the way in which these participants spoke about their schooled reading, which was embedded in a discourse of expectation and judgement.

To take this point further, these parents also spoke about their aims and purposes in maintaining shared reading, which was often focussed on gaining enjoyment. To stay with Hadra for the moment, when asked to talk about the reasons why she and her husband engaged in shared reading practices with their daughter she told us:

> To be honest, at the moment, importance in terms of how her reading is and how good she is with it, it doesn't come into it. I think, that's not why we do it. We do it because she enjoys it and it's something we can do together.

As discussed at length in Chapter 6, many parents across the study reported that what they ultimately wanted to achieve from shared reading activity was for their child to enjoy the experience. This underlines the finding that these participants, who had not enjoyed reading for themselves, were not only enjoying reading to their children but appreciated the fact that the purpose of this reading was to enjoy the experience together, rather than focus on decoding print. This was also evident in Bina's interview who stated that both she and her husband 'have the same kind of end goal' for shared reading, 'which is to make her (daughter) laugh'. This again shows that these parents viewed shared reading as an activity to be carried out with the main purpose of promoting enjoyment rather than achieving proficiency in reading.

This is significant because when asked to talk about their own personal relationship with reading, these parents described a range of proficiency judgements that were attached to schooled reading, which included judgements from teachers and peers on their ability to decode text with accuracy and read aloud with fluency. They also judged themselves against other people who enjoyed reading ('I'm the only one on this Earth who doesn't like reading'). In contrast, the reading that these parents described doing with their children was not only a very different experience from their own schooled reading, but actually seemed to carry a different definition of what 'reading' actually is. These parents were describing an activity that was not forced, that did not carry proficiency judgement, where enjoyment was prioritised and, importantly, included factors such as talking to their child and enjoying spending time together. This may very well explain why these parents succeeded in developing a positive reading relationship with their children despite the fact that they had a poor relationship with reading them-selves. This is a very positive finding; however, the data also suggested that in some cases, the parents not only developed a good reading relationship with their children, but that their own relationships with reading improved as a result of this as now discussed.

Shared reading: supporting parents' own reading

It was clear from the data that all of the parents who reported that they did not enjoy reading for themselves all went on to report that they enjoyed reading with their children. As discussed above, we argue that this may be because reading, within a shared reading context, was very different to the reading that these parents had previously experienced. However, the data also showed that some of these parents became more engaged with certain aspects of reading in general as a result of their shared reading interactions.

This was evident in Latika's interview. Having told us that she found all books to be 'boring' while at school, and still does not enjoy books now she is an adult, Latika told us that she is now getting to know lots of stories through the context of reading with her daughter. She went on to report that not only does her daughter enjoy shared reading, but stated: 'I'm learning now, there's so many things, there are so many stories I've read now, which I have never read in my life before'. Latika is making the point that she is an active participant in the shared reading relationship and is 'learning' alongside her child. She then went on to make the point that it is because she and her daughter read 'every day' that she herself has come to read 'so many stories', which she sees as a benefit to herself as well as her daughter.

Similarly, Fiona also spoke of the fact that it was the routine of everyday life with young children that encouraged her to read. Having initially reported that when she was in her twenties, it 'didn't enter my spectrum to think about reading books', Fiona spoke about the fact that having children meant she was 'at home a lot more' and this encouraged her 'to read a bit more', both with her children and for herself. We can see that by engaging with books through the context of shared reading, Fiona was encouraged to read books for herself, which was not something that she had previously considered doing.

Finally Natalie, who reported that she had found reading in school particularly stressful, talked in detail about the ways in which her own relationship with books had developed as a consequence of her shared reading activity with her children. She stated:

> I think I enjoy reading more now with the kids because I'm excited to do different things with them, thinking of things I could do with the book, things I could get them doing while I'm reading the book. Which is good because I wasn't really a book reader... And I'm learning about new authors as well, like it wasn't something that I was that interested in so it's nice, now I look at the stories and I'm looking for more books that that author's wrote that I think he might enjoy. I never used to do that – just got books that looked good on a cover.

There are so many points being raised in this statement that illustrate the complex ways in which Natalie's relationship with reading has grown from sharing books with her children. Having been someone who 'wasn't really a book reader', Natalie is now using the kind of strategies that experienced readers use to select books, such as 'learning about new authors' and finding more books that a particular author has written. In addition, Natalie speaks of being 'excited' by the different things that she can do with her children with the book, suggesting that she now has a very different relationship with books compared to when she was younger. Interestingly, when asked directly about her own confidence in reading now, Natalie was in no doubt that reading with her children had improved her own confidence in reading. She reported:

> I feel okay. I've picked it up more as I've gone along. I'm more confident now with the kids than I was when I was younger. I think I'm good at reading now, I hope so.

What we can see from this data is that these parents, who stated that they had not have a good relationship with reading themselves, not only went on to enjoy reading with their children, but actually reported that their own relationship with reading had strengthened as a direct result of their shared reading interactions. We know that some young people do not enjoy reading for themselves and may find aspects of the school discourse, such as being made to read aloud in class, particularly discouraging. However, this data suggests that there is no reason to assume that this will make these parents less likely to read with their own children. On the contrary, this data suggests that some parents might find that their own relationship with reading improves as a direct consequence of the shared reading activity they perform with their children.

Conclusion

This chapter has reported the encouraging, yet somewhat unexpected finding, that the parents in this study who had identified themselves as having a poor personal relationship with reading went on to develop positive shared reading relationships with their children. While this is a pleasing and welcome finding, it would be highly naïve to assume that this is the case for all parents who have struggled with reading themselves at school or who do not enjoy reading for themselves. This is particularly important given that research has shown that vast numbers of young people leave school each year with a poor identity of themselves as a reader (Alvermann, 2001), and/or have been identified as 'unsuccessful' in literacy-based assessment (Greenleaf & Hinchman, 2009). Yet, in taking the time to understand the nature and indeed complexity of shared reading relationships in families, the Shared Reading Project has significant implications for the ways in which educationalists and other professionals who work with families, can offer support, especially when the parents report that they have not enjoyed a positive relationship with reading themselves.

As discussed at various points in this book, while there is a substantial amount of literature on reading in the home that has explored what parents do, and why it is beneficial (Clark & Hawkins, 2010; Gjems, 2010; Mullan, 2010), very little research has attempted to understand the nature of shared reading relationships. Moreover, as discussed in detail in this book, the Shared Reading Project has shown that these practices are highly individual and unique to the social and cultural context of the family. For example, we have seen how shared reading activities were often led by the children, rather than by the parents themselves. This has very important implications for reading intervention in general; having established that many reading interventions are not successful (Justice et al., 2015; Justice, Skibbe et al., 2011), this study suggests that this may be because reading interventions rarely acknowledge the unique nature of family reading practices, and the factors that motivate and discourage parents from reading with their children.

In understanding the uniqueness of individual reading relationships, data from this study has shown that the construct of 'reading', within their shared reading relationships with their children, was very different from the ways in which reading was defined in school for these participants. For many of the parents in this study who reported a poor personal relationship with reading, it appeared that their own reading carried a set of proficiency judgements, determined by educational discourses and societal expectation; however, this was not the case with their shared reading activity with their children. This was not 'forced' and did not carry proficiency judgement. Reading was seen as a very flexible construct, which included talking and telling stories. Above all, parents seemed to value the space it provided for them to enjoy protected time with their children and for all parties to enjoy the activity.

This suggests that practitioners who are supporting families in initiating and maintaining shared reading practices in the home, need to recognise that parents not only have different relationships with reading themselves, but that this may have an impact on how they have come to define reading. In turn, these definitions may influence how parents view shared reading with their children. By drawing on this, and the other main findings discussed in the last four chapters of this book, the next chapter looks specifically at the implications of these findings for practice. In particular, we consider how practitioners from within various disciplines and professions can support all families in gaining enjoyment from reading regularly with their children at home.

9

WORKING WITH FAMILIES TO PROMOTE SHARED READING

So what have we come to understand about shared reading in families? Perhaps the most prominent finding is that this is a not a straightforward question to answer! Through our conversations with the parents participating in this project, we have learned that families read in different ways, for different purposes and with different motivations. Recognising that this is the case is probably one of the most fundamental, yet important points to emerge from this book, as this has major implications for how parents may be encouraged and supported in reading with their children.

The Shared Reading project explored the views and practices of 29 families, many of whom live in areas of disadvantage, through the context of in-depth interviews. While it would be foolish to suggest that these families represented a wider population as such, the themes within the data do have substantial implications for the ways in which practitioners work with many different families. By taking time to talk to these parents about their beliefs, practices, motivations and struggles, we came to understand how shared reading in the home may differ substantially from dominant discourses about reading which reside within school contexts.

As we approach the end of this book, this chapter summarises the main findings from this study and discusses the implications of these. In doing so, the chapter turns to the role of practitioners (by using the term 'practitioner' we refer to all those who may work with families in a professional capacity) and explores the ways in which parents may be encouraged to begin or maintain shared reading with their children. This research has shown that if we want to support parents in reading with their children, we need to begin with the family. The first part of this chapter therefore consolidates the main research findings before showing what this means for practitioners working with families.

What is shared reading in families?

One major aim of this study was to understand the features of shared reading within the families who participated in this study – or to put this another way, to explore what it looked like. Parents spoke to us with enthusiasm about the unique and individual ways in which they read with their children. They also spoke about their goals and motivations for reading as well as their concerns and difficulties. As researchers, we were in the highly privileged position of being allowed to learn how shared reading operated within individual families as well as being witness to the 'bigger picture' which emerged across the cohort as a whole. This picture told its own story about shared reading within a group of families, many of whom were living in relative disadvantage. Somewhat conveniently, this picture can be understood in terms of the 'Four T's', these being text, talk, time and togetherness.

Text

In the opening chapter of this book we presented a definition for the term 'shared reading'. We stated our claim that the term describes an activity where a child is engaged in focusing on a text with another person (usually an adult) for a sustained period of time. Given that this joint attention on a text will often result in some kind of 'shared construction of meaning' (Yuill & Martin, 2016), this suggests that shared reading is not just about sharing a text but engaging in the shared generation of meaning which arises from the event. The project data indicated that this was very much the case for the families in this study. As the last four chapters have clearly shown, shared reading was, for many of the families, a dynamic activity that was surrounded by talk, laughter and play. Parents gave animated accounts of their individual shared reading activities, where they put on different voices, told their own stories or sang songs.

What became increasingly clear as we spent time with the whole dataset was that parents used texts in different ways to engage their children in meaningful literacy events. Indeed, words in books were read, and pictures were discussed, but many of the parents in this study also seemed happy to divert from the text and add their own narratives. In some cases this took the form of a parent inserting their child's name into the narrative, while others created new endings for a story or added detail to the printed text from their own imagination. Interestingly, when talking about shared reading some parents spoke naturally about creating their own stories and not using a text at all. In other words, many of the parents in this study seemed to use texts in whatever manner was most likely to provoke the engagement of their individual child.

So what does this say about the role of text within shared reading? In Chapter 1 we discussed the fact that advancements in technology means that the term 'text' now includes digital as well as paper-based media (Bearne, 2003). We also know that many children are competent users of digital technology even before they start school (Marsh, 2005), which has led many scholars to argue (rightly in our view!) that schools do children a disservice by emphasising the decoding of print in paper-based books and fail to acknowledge the importance of digital texts within children's lives (Carrington & Robinson, 2009; Marsh et al., 2005). As we have pointed out elsewhere in this book, the parents in this study tended to talk largely about paper-based books and rarely spoke about using digital texts during shared reading activity. However, the results of this study suggest that in understanding shared reading with young children in homes, there is little to be gained from focusing on the actual texts that were used, but much to be gained from understanding how parents *used* texts, which tended to be flexible and responsive to the needs of their child.

As we have demonstrated, many of the parents in this study seemed to use the text as a catalyst to facilitate communication and engagement with their children. Of course, some parents did speak fondly about particular texts, such as certain books that they had enjoyed themselves when they were children; however, in describing their own shared reading activities with their children the emphasis was usually on their need to see their child enjoy the experience and engage with the activity. What is more, given that parents used texts flexibly in their shared reading activities, or in some cases did not use a physical text at all, this again places emphasis on the role of the text as a facilitator of a communicative exchange where shared meaning is generated, whether it be a paper-based book, screen text, picture or any other type of text.

Talk

As discussed above, one of the salient features of shared reading for these families was that it provided an opportunity for parent and child to communicate with each other. In particular parents valued the space that shared reading created for them to talk with their children. Many of the comments we received from parents in relation to this are echoed in Natalie's words when she said that conversation with her son 'goes off books', meaning that the book was the vehicle for the talk that was generated during the activity. This was further clarified when she went on to say, 'just because we've got books in our hand, we talk about the rest of the day'. Indeed, many of the parents in this study spoke of shared reading as a place where they would talk with their children about a whole variety of things such as what they had both done that day.

As explained in Chapter 8, the data indicated that shared reading with young children appeared to carry a particular definition of 'reading' that differed substantially from schooled definitions. Shared reading was seen to be flexible, open-ended and free, meaning that crucially it contained space for talk. The talk may have been focused on the text and parents did use the content of texts to activate dialogue; however, parents also used shared reading as a space to simply talk with their child about anything that was going on in their lives.

The talk that was generated from shared reading activity was not always parent–child conversation. Sometimes parents used shared reading as an opportunity to allow their voices to soothe or comfort children; this may have happened if the child was tired or unwell for example. In these cases parents told us that they were not expecting their children to respond within the activity, but rather they were reading with the express purposes of allowing their child to hear their voice. Some participants told us that they had read to their children since they were babies for this very reason – a few participants even reported that they had read to their children before they were born. This again shows how shared reading provided a unique space for parents to interact with their children in a manner that may not otherwise have been possible.

Time

Linking with the above, when asked to talk about reading with their children in the home, many of the parents told us that they valued the fact that shared reading provided protected time for them to spend with their children. For some this was associated with a routine, such as a bedtime routine, while other parents told us that shared reading could happen at any time of the day. Whatever the case, many parents used expressions such as 'our time' or 'his/her time' to describe their shared reading activity.

What is more, when asked about the value of shared reading, it was common for parents to talk about 'spending time' with their child, claiming that this was one of the most important outcomes of the activity. While some parents did talk about the value of shared reading in terms of factors such as child learning, it was far more common for the parents in this study to speak of valuing the time they were spending with their child. As has been emphasised in the above two sections, this time was cherished as it provided an opportunity for parent and child to enjoy each other's company and communicate with one another. This leads us to the next feature of shared reading identified in this study, which we have chosen to call 'togetherness'.

Togetherness

Almost every parent in the study spoke about shared reading as an opportunity for them to develop their relationship with their child; while many parents used the term 'bonding', others spoke about 'being close' being 'intimate' or having a 'connection'. The bond that was shared between parent and child during shared reading appeared to run in both directions, with parents telling us that they were able to bond with their child and their child would bond with them. While it stands to reason that many other activities could facilitate bonding between parent and child, such as watching a television programme together, sharing a meal or carrying out a household task, the data suggested that shared reading offered a special affordance in this respect. This may well be because of the way that shared reading brought the four T's together – parents valued the protected *time* that was often built into their day, to read with their child, where they would focus *together* on a *text*. The joint attention on a *text* facilitated a quality of *talk* to emerge, which in turn brought parent and child closer *together*.

What is more, the parents in this study also spoke about the physical connections that they made with their child during shared reading activity. Drawing on Mason's concept of 'sensory affinity' we began to see how shared reading was a highly sensory experience for many of the families. The joint focus on a text often resulted in parent and child being physically close together ('dead cuddle' 'snuggle in'), hearing each other ('intently listen' 'we chat about what's happening in the pictures'), seeing each other ('you can see him taking it in') and taking in the scent of one another ('he's all bathed and fresh and I can get in bed with him'). This again demonstrates why shared reading appeared to offer a special opportunity for parent and child to bond together; parents described an interaction with their child that enacted the senses allowing them to see, touch, hear and smell their child, all of which merged together to promote bonding.

Why do parents read with their children?

One of the drivers for the research reported in this book was to understand potential barriers to shared reading, with a view to finding ways to support families in overcoming these barriers; however, the project findings suggested that this was not the most useful way to think about shared reading in families. Rather than beginning with the concept of understanding why shared reading might not take place, the project data indicated that there was much to learn about what shared reading actually looked like (as described above) and how it functioned within the realm of everyday family practice. This, in turn, allowed us to consider the factors that may be especially important for parents if shared reading is to be initiated and maintained in homes.

One of the most striking findings from this study was the vital role that enjoyment played in shared reading activity. Almost all of the parents in this study spoke about the fact that they enjoyed reading with their child, but this enjoyment was highly individual. Some parents spoke about enjoying spending time with their children and the pleasure they found in being close and bonding with their child. Given that shared reading appeared to provide a special opportunity for this to happen, as demonstrated above, it is not surprising that some parents read with their children because they enjoyed having this time to be close to their child. For others, their enjoyment was linked to other parental motivations for reading; for example, if parents spoke about using shared reading to create a calm and quiet atmosphere, they seemed to enjoy reading quietly with their child where they could both 'relax' or 'settle'. Others however spoke of shared reading in terms of something that was altogether more stimulating, making reference to 'silly voices', laughter and noise; in these situations parents seemed to enjoy having fun with their child.

The parents in this study read with their children because they enjoyed it; indeed, this is not a surprise as previous research has identified 'enjoying reading' as a parental goal of shared reading activity (Audet et al., 2008); however, this only begins to explain the role of enjoyment within the shared reading relationship. As highlighted in Chapter 6, parents' enjoyment of shared reading was often closely related to the feedback they received from their children. When parents could see that their child was enjoying the activity, this in turn enhanced the parents' enjoyment and subsequent motivation to carry on with shared reading activity. We have termed this process the 'cycle of reciprocity' (see Figure 7.1 in Chapter 7), where the feedback from the child has a clear influence on the maintenance of further shared reading events. Importantly though, the consequence of this cycle meant that if some parents did not receive feedback to indicate that their child was enjoying the activity, they reported that they would be far less likely to initiate further shared reading activities. In fact, some parents were quite clear that they would not carry on reading with their child if their child did not appear to be enjoying it, as child enjoyment was a major motivation for doing shared reading.

While enjoyment of shared reading remained a central concern for most of the parents in this study, the data also indicated that this was linked to concerns for child learning. As explained in Chapter 6, it was not the original intention of this study to compare the participants with one another, but it did become clear that there was a difference in how some of the families from lower income groups perceived child learning within shared reading, in comparison with some families who were in a higher income bracket. Most of the families across the whole dataset told us that child enjoyment should be a key aim of shared reading activity; however, families from within lower income brackets were more inclined to report that they needed to see evidence of their child's enjoyment in order to maintain shared reading activity. What is more, some of these families went on to state that while the goal of shared reading was enjoyment, they were also aware that the activity was simultaneously promoting an aspect of their child's learning. Seeing evidence of this learning further encouraged the parents to enjoy shared reading with their child, therefore strengthening the cycle of reciprocity. In contrast, while parents from within a higher income bracket also stated that child enjoyment should be a main goal of shared reading, some of these parents also reported that another goal of shared reading was to promote learning – especially language development. This suggests that these parents may be less dependent on gaining positive feedback from their children given that they were also motivated to read to their children because they believed it would support their child's learning.

This also has implications for reading with babies. While some of the parents in this study did say that they had read to their children since they were babies, many others stated that they either did not do this, or had stopped trying because they felt that their child was 'not ready'. This is understandable given that babies are unlikely to provide the kind of feedback that many of the parents in this study seemed to need in order to initiate and maintain shared reading activity. However, we do know that babies and toddlers are born with intrinsic curiosity and innate needs for stimulation which adults can support in various ways (Gammage, 2006; Meltzoff & Moore, 1999; Nutbrown & Page, 2008), and that reading to babies is one effective way in which to provide this support.

To boil this down, parents appear to read with their children because it is enjoyable for themselves and their children, and this has a number of implications for practitioners working with families as discussed in the second part of this chapter; however, the project data suggested that parents read with their children for other reasons. Some parents in this study reported that they read with their children for purposes of child learning, which included language development, engagement with books, learning about the world in general and moral development. As mentioned above, the parents in this study who were within a higher income bracket were more likely to state that child learning was a goal of shared reading, than the parents within lower income brackets. This in no way suggests that parents within lower income brackets did not care about learning – to the contrary parents spoke with great concern about their children's education. But these parents were less likely to state that one of their goals for shared reading was for their child to learn. In sum, the project data showed that all of the parents in this study clearly wanted their children to learn, but few appeared to prioritise child learning as a main motivation for shared reading. Those who did say that they read with their children to promote learning were more likely to come from within higher income brackets, but it is fair to say that they also tended to prioritise enjoyment as a goal for shared reading above child learning.

As discussed in Chapter 3, previous research has tried to establish parental goals for shared reading, concluding that parents read for a variety of reasons such as to 'stimulate development', 'bond with their child', 'soothe their child', 'foster reading' and 'enjoy reading' (Audet et al., 2008). The parents in the Shared Reading Project certainly spoke of all these factors in relation to the reasons why they read with their children, but this was by no means the end of the story. Firstly as demonstrated above, we have learned that factors such as 'enjoyment' are highly complex and are embedded in a cycle of reciprocal exchange, which emphasises the importance of child feedback for many parents if shared reading is likely to be maintained. Secondly, the data suggested that for many families, shared reading was first and foremost an everyday family practice. Of course, parents may have had particular reasons for maintaining the practice, such as to promote bonding with their child, but it is important to recognise the crucial role that shared reading played in making up the fabric of everyday family life.

For example, we saw in Chapter 5 how shared reading was not only part of everyday family practice but had a role in developing and managing aspects of daily life. We saw how shared reading was used as a tool to establish routines and bring structure and shape to the day, especially with pre-school age children. In addition it was also used to help parents to navigate and manage some of the complexities of everyday life, such as to teach their child about values or to instil aspects of identity that were important to their individual family. This shows why it is naïve to suggest that anyone can simply encourage parents to read with their children as this is to vastly underestimate the role of the family within the process. This research has shown that shared reading is a complex phenomenon, moulded by the ebb and flow of everyday life and shaped by the cultural context of the individual family. What is more, the project data also indicated that the children were themselves central to the maintenance of shared reading activity.

Many of the parents in this study reported that they often read with their children because their child wanted to read. Parents told us that their children regularly initiated the activity, by bringing books to their parents or asking to be read to. Moreover these children also seemed to have a major role in directing how shared reading would happen (e.g. diverting from the text or bringing play into the activity), when it would happen (for example, asking to read during the day or in the bath) and what was to be shared (e.g. determining which book or page of a book would be read). This is critical because it not only shows how children can exert considerable agency within the process, but it also demonstrates the importance of the child's role in motivating parents to read or sustain shared reading activity with their children, given that parents told us that they would usually read with their children simply because their child.

In summary, this study has revealed that parents' motivations for shared reading are far more complex – and indeed far more interesting – than previous research has suggested. While parents may well have specific goals for shared reading, such as to encourage a love of books or to bond with their child, shared reading often happened in these homes because it was part of everyday family life. Parents read with their children because they enjoyed it, their children enjoyed it and because their children asked to be read to. What is more, it also became increasingly evident that in order to understand why parents read with their children, it was necessary to focus on the question of what shared reading does *for* the family, as now discussed.

What does shared reading do for families?

As discussed above, shared reading had a role in developing and managing aspects of family life such as helping to establish and embed routines into the day. It was not surprising to find that parents would often use shared reading at bedtime to settle their children and signal the end of the day; parents who did this spoke with conviction of the importance of shared reading as part of the bedtime routine, often claiming that their children would simply not go to sleep if they didn't read together at night. However, shared reading was also used to help manage aspects of the day, such as ensuring that each parent, within two parent families, got to spend time with the child at some point in the day, or that each child in the family got to spend some time on their own with a parent. Shared reading was also used to bring calm to fractious moments, and to inject fun and entertainment into others. What became clear as we became increasingly close to the dataset as a whole was that the ways in which parents used shared reading to manage family life was specific to the everyday needs, routines and practices of individual families.

Shared reading was used in families to support the practical management of everyday life, but we also found that it provided other benefits for families that were not immediately so apparent. In particular we found that shared reading provided opportunities for families to 'display' (Finch, 2007) their agency and indeed 'familyness' to each other and the outside world. For example, some parents told us that they started reading to their children from a young age because it was a comfort to them to know that they were carrying out a customary parent–child activity. This helped these parents to display their parenting to themselves as well as others, which helped affirm that they were 'doing family' (Finch, 2007), which in turn provided comfort and pleasure. In other examples (see Amy's story discussed in Chapter 5) shared reading allowed people who were not blood relations, such as a new partner, to enter the family unit and display that they were now part of this family, through the manifestation of this family activity. In brief, shared reading provided families with the means to display to themselves and the outside world that they are a family and 'it works' (Finch, 2007: 73).

The final major finding in this study, with regard to the benefits of shared reading for families, related to the parents' own relationship with reading. We had a number of questions in mind as we set out on this study and one of these was to investigate if having a seemingly poor personal relationship with reading could inhibit parents in reading aloud with their own children. The data from this study clearly showed that this was not the case for the parents in this study. As explained in Chapter 8, about a third of the parents in this study reported that they did not enjoy reading for themselves, or had had what might be regarded as a 'poor' relationship with reading when they were a child, yet they all went on to develop strong shared reading relationships with their own children. Moreover, in a number of cases, parents reported that their own relationship with reading had strengthened as a direct consequence of their shared reading interactions with their children.

We know that some young people do not enjoy reading for themselves and may find aspects of the school discourse, such as being made to read aloud in class, particularly discouraging. This is reflected in research that has shown that large numbers of young people leave school each year with a poor sense of identity of themselves as a reader (Alvermann, 2001), and/or have been identified as 'unsuccessful' in literacy-based assessment (Greenleaf & Hinchman, 2009). Yet this study has shown that there is no reason to assume that this will make these individuals less likely to read with their own children, given the fact that shared reading with young children appears to carry a very different definition of 'reading' to that offered by the school discourse. As highlighted at the beginning of this chapter shared reading with young children in the home can be understood in terms of the Four T's; flexibility in how *texts* are used, space to generate a quality of *talk* between parent and child, an opportunity to spend protected *time* with a child and the generation of a sense of *togetherness* that was characterised by a warm sensory exchange. What is more, for some of the parents in this study, reading within this construct appeared to result in these parents having an improved personal relationship with reading for themselves.

Shared reading interventions

It is not unusual to find interventions that have been designed with the express purpose of encouraging parents to read with their children. Yet research has suggested that such interventions are not always successful. For example, Justice et al. (2015: 1852) argued that:

> It is most certainly the case that implementation of shared-reading interventions by caregivers within the home environment does not always reach the levels intended by the intervention developers.

As a result, Justice et al. (2015) set out to identify barriers affecting caregivers' implementation of shared-reading interventions with their children with language impairment, concluding that the reasons why caregivers did not implement the intervention as designed related to 'time pressures', 'difficulty with reading', 'discomfort with reading' and 'lack of awareness of reading benefits'. When we consider these factors, in the light of findings from the Shared Reading Project, what becomes immediately apparent is that these are barriers to the implementation of an intervention, rather than barriers to shared reading as such.

This raises serious questions about the extent to which these interventions fitted with the everyday practices of the families involved. As we have seen repeatedly in this book, shared reading in families cannot be understood in isolation from the everydayness of family life, culture and practice. The parents in our study told us that they read with their children because it worked for them in their homes. For many of the parents, this was the ultimate driving force in maintaining shared reading activity, and if it did not work then they would not do it. If, therefore, an intervention does not fit within the construct of the family's everyday life, or is asking parents to behave in a manner that is not natural for them and their children, then it is not surprising to hear that caregivers are not implementing the intervention activities as the developers had hoped.

What is more, these perceived barriers are also suggesting a degree of judgement on the part of those involved in the creation of the intervention. Parents are being described as having 'a lack of awareness' about the benefits of shared reading, together with having 'difficulty' or 'discomfort' in reading. Yet the project data suggests that such perceptions may be seriously misguided. By describing parents in this way, shared reading is being situated within a narrow discourse that privileges certain constructions of reading, usually attached to a school-focused agenda. Within this discourse, parents are constructed as being unknowing and unable. However, findings from the Shared Reading Project strongly refutes this. Findings suggest that when we begin with the family, and take time to understand how shared reading operates within the home, we can learn much about the skill, confidence, motivation and agency of parents, including those who may have not enjoyed reading for themselves. The remainder of this chapter now considers exactly how the findings from this study can be used by practitioners working with families, to encourage and support the development of shared reading activity in the home.

Implications for practitioners working with families

There are a number of different individuals and organisations who work with families with young children; these could include teachers, child care workers, social workers, health care practitioners, family support workers, family therapists, psychologists and those within the legal profession. This list is not exhaustive and may of course include a wide variety of other practitioners, together with all those who may interact with families in a less formal capacity such as friends, family and neighbours. The purpose of this section is to offer guidance, on the basis of the findings from the Shared Reading Project, to all those who may be in a position to support families in initiating and maintaining shared reading in their homes. For the purposes of this chapter the term 'practitioners' will be used to describe these individuals.

Who is the expert?

We know that shared reading is beneficial for children with a number of studies over the years linking shared reading with skills in literacy and language as well as literacy appreciation (Martin-Chang & Gould, 2012; de

Jong, Mol & Bus, 2009; Snow, 1994). We also know that it has numerous other benefits, many of which have been clearly manifest in the data presented in this book. Shared reading provides an opportunity for parent and child to spend protected time together, bonding, talking, enjoying each other's company and participating in a shared sensory experience. Practitioners can and should support families by encouraging shared reading, but how practitioners perceive themselves in relation to the families with whom they are working must be considered.

In a study of parents' attitudes towards parenting education, Holloway and Pimlott-Wilson (2012: 94) argue that developments in parenting education have led to 'the professionalization of parenting', meaning that 'parenting has been reframed from a "personal family relationship" to "a technical exercise— something that you can either get right or wrong" (Gillies, 2010, p. 44)'. Holloway and Pimlott-Wilson (2012: 94) go on to stress that even more worrying is the concern that concepts of 'good parenting'; therefore, getting it 'right', are not neutral, evident in the fact that policy has been shaped by middle-class values, meaning that working-class parents are being encouraged 'to behave in middle class ways' (James, 2009; Klett-Davies, 2010). This has major implications for practitioners who are working with families to encourage shared reading.

As the data in this book has repeatedly shown, for many of the families in this study, and particularly those living in disadvantage, shared reading was not perceived as a chore, or something that had to be fitted into the day for reasons of educational endeavour. Rather parents told us that they read with their children because it was enjoyable, and as a result it became part of everyday family practice. This suggests that if we want to encourage shared reading, we need to begin with what the family already does, already enjoys and already wants. Therefore practitioners working with families to encourage shared reading need to recognise from the outset that while they may have expertise in areas related to their own profession, the experts in being this family are this family.

What works for the family

It is not uncommon for parents to receive advice from professional services about reading with their children. This often takes the form of encouraging parents to read with their children at bedtimes (see, e.g., Booktrust's 'Bath Book Bed' campaign). As we saw in Chapter 5, many parents in this study told us that they not only read with their children at bedtime but they really valued the routine. Some parents even claimed that bedtime stories had become an essential feature within their day, evident in comments such as 'I don't think anyone would sleep if we didn't have books' (Hadra). There is no doubt that for some families, the introduction of a bedtime routine, which includes a bedtime story, may be enormously beneficial, and practitioners may well find that they can support families in establishing such a routine. However, it would be dangerous for practitioners to suggest that bedtime reading is 'the right' thing for all families to do. Consequently this would lead to the assertion that if parents were not reading to their children at night, they were somehow getting it 'wrong', and failing in an aspect of their parenting. Given that it has been well documented that activities such as bedtime stories are aligned with middle-class values (Heath, 1982; Brooker, 2002; Nichols, 2000) this indicates a further need for caution in how practitioners present such advice.

Together this suggests that an important role for practitioners is to help parents to reflect on their own individual family lives and encourage them to find ways of embedding regular shared reading activity into their existing family practices. In other words, parents should be supported and encouraged to read with their children in ways, and at times that work for their own individual family. Practitioners should recognise that it can be empowering for parents to be hear that in working out what works best for their own family, they are indeed getting 'it right'. This might mean that shared reading happens at bedtime, but it might also mean that it happens at other times of the day, perhaps once other family members have gone to work or school and a parent has some time alone with a younger child.

For some families, rather than focusing on shared reading as an activity that *should* take place to support a child's language and literacy development, it might be more helpful for a practitioner to focus on the notion of *allowing* shared reading to work for the family. Data from the project clearly showed that parents used shared reading to structure and manage aspects of daily life. The parents in this study used it to establish routines, to calm and settle, to entertain, to teach and to create space. By talking to parents about their daily lives including struggles, concerns, plans and hopes, practitioners may be able to help parents to use shared reading to support their everyday family lives. For example, given the potential of shared reading to help parents and children bond together, shared reading may be used to help a parent develop their relationship with their child, or to help a new partner to connect with a child. It may be used to help a parent to address a difficult topic with a child, or to simply entertain at salient points in the day.

In brief, while it is useful for parents to know that shared reading has educational benefits for children, an emphasis on this alone may do little to help some parents to embed shared reading into their everyday family lives. But by inviting parents to consider the structure of their own lives and then, on the basis of this, helping parents to use shared reading to enhance and manage family life, practitioners may find that they can encourage parents to read with their children in ways that not only fit with their family life but also supports its individual members.

Helping parents to enjoy shared reading

One of the most striking findings from the project was the huge role that enjoyment played in the maintenance of shared reading activity. Parents told us time and again that the main reason they read with their children was because it was enjoyable. This enjoyment was embedded in what we have called a cycle of reciprocity, where parents' enjoyment was triggered by their gaining positive feedback from their child. This in turn encouraged the parents to keep reading with their children, and as a result the activity continued.

Helping parents to enjoy reading with their children is probably one of the most important aims for practitioners. Given the importance of the reciprocal relationship between parent and child, practitioners should talk to parents about finding a time that they can read with their child where they are unlikely to be disturbed or distracted by other people or other events. Of course, for some parents with multiple children, it may be simply impossible to spend protected time with each child individually, but what we have learned from the data in this study is that spending time reading with an individual child seemed to be especially enjoyable for both parent and child.

Parents should also be encouraged to find ways of enhancing enjoyment for themselves, depending on what works for them and their children. For example, a typical scenario may be that a parent is trying to read a book from start to finish, but the child wants to deviate from the text. The parent may get frustrated and feel that the child is not interested in reading. In a case like this, practitioners could perhaps suggest that parents allow themselves to be led by the child and use this as an opportunity to focus on having fun with the child rather than completing a particular text. In this respect, practitioners can really support parents by simply giving them 'permission' to prioritise enjoyment as an aim for shared reading. For example, if a parent is struggling to hold their child's attention, practitioners can suggest that their goal for the next event is to make their child laugh. Similarly, a goal may be to find something new in a picture or to encourage the child to talk. The purpose of this section is not to prescribe a definitive list of things practitioners should do, but rather to encourage practitioners to work with parents to find ways of increasing the enjoyment of shared reading activity for the individual family.

That said, the project data strongly suggested that the parents in this study had personal connections with the texts they were reading with their children, and the parents' enjoyment of shared reading seemed to be enhanced if they liked the text they were reading. Certainly, practitioners can support parental enjoyment of reading by encouraging parents to read texts that they enjoy reading themselves. If a parent is enjoying reading a text, they are more likely to engage their child in the event and therefore promote child enjoyment. Obviously some practitioners will be better placed than others to recommend specific texts, but where this is possible this should again be made with the needs of the individual family in mind. Whatever the case, it is important to prioritise enjoyment, and support parents in finding texts that they will enjoy reading with their children.

Managing child feedback

While it is fair to say that most of the parents in this study did read with their children, they also spoke openly about the factors that had inhibited shared reading. What became abundantly clear was that, in particular, a lack of positive feedback from their child made it difficult for parents to maintain shared reading activity. This ties closely with the points raised above about the importance of enjoyment within the shared reading event – the more a parent receives feedback from their child to show that they are enjoying the activity, the more parents are motivated to initiate further activity. But what does this mean for parents who are not receiving what they perceive to be positive feedback? How can practitioners help in these cases?

As described above, one important strategy is to help the parent to make the activity enjoyable for the child. For example, parents may be encouraged to bring components of play to the activity, or to include some songs or nursery rhymes. They might be encouraged to bring an element of surprise to the story, or say something silly that will make the child laugh. Of course, the extent to which this will be effective will depend very much on the individual parent and their own goals for the activity. However, it is possible that a parent may feel that in enacting the above, they are no longer 'reading' with their child which could cause new frustrations, but this is where practitioners can stress that shared reading with young children does not need to resemble 'schooled' constructions of reading that tend to be focused on decoding print; this is discussed in more detail in the next chapter. As the findings from this study have shown, shared reading with young children is not just about reading words in a book, but is about talking, laughing, bonding and sharing. Helping parents to understand that all of these factors are beneficial for children will hopefully give parents the confidence to carry out shared reading in ways that suit them and their children, and will result in positive feedback from the child.

What we also learned from the parents in this study is that what was perceived to be an absence of feedback also made it difficult for parents to read with their children, often because parents believed that this meant that their child was 'not ready' to be read to. This has particular implications for reading with babies, given that very young infants are unlikely to be able to demonstrate the kind of enjoyment and engagement that will be evident with an older child. Encouraging parents to read with babies may be a challenge, especially if this is not something that has traditionally taken place within the parents' home culture. However, practitioners can still talk to parents about the benefits of reading to babies, and the value of having an activity that allows the parent to talk directly to the baby. If a parent feels uncomfortable using a book with such a small child, then practitioners can suggest using other props such as a toy or a picture to focus the parent–child activity and centre the talk. What is more, establishing parent–child reading with a baby can help to establish shared reading as part of everyday family practice, which sets the scene for future shared reading activity.

Finally, the project data also suggested that, in many cases, parents read with their children because their children were asking to be read to. In other words, much of the reading that happened did so because the activity was being initiated by the child. This suggests that practitioners may also want to talk to parents about the child's role in the activity. For example, if a parent is reporting that their child appears disinterested in reading, then it would be wise to suggest that the parent encourages the child to take an active role in the process, perhaps by encouraging the child to choose what is to be read and/or how it is to be read. Parents may find that by explicitly allowing or encouraging their child to lead the activity, they become more engaged and therefore more likely to offer positive feedback.

Conclusion

This chapter began with a summary of the main findings drawn from the Shared Reading Project. We showed how shared reading in homes can be understood as a social practice which is defined by the Four T's of text, talk, time and togetherness; we saw how shared reading was characterised by flexibility in how *texts* are used, space to generate a quality of *talk* between parent and child, an opportunity to spend protected *time* with a child and the generation of a sense of *togetherness* that was characterised by a warm sensory exchange. We have learned that parents read with their children because they enjoyed it and their children enjoyed it, and as a result it became part of everyday family practice. Shared reading was also seen to have a number of benefits for the family; while parents did talk about the educational benefits for their children, they also spoke of the role shared reading played in developing and managing aspects of family life such as helping to establish and embed routines into the day. In addition, shared reading offered families an avenue through which to display their parenting, which helped to affirm that they were successfully 'doing family'.

In the introduction to this book, we attempted to find a definition for the term 'reading', arguing that the schooling system is responsible for how many of us come to define what reading is, and how we perceive ourselves as readers. Yet what we have found in this study, as summarised in this chapter, is that 'reading', within a shared reading context in the home, looks quite different to the ways in which reading might appear within a schooled context. This is important as we consider ways in which parents can be supported in reading with their children in the home. On the basis of findings drawn from the Shared Reading Project, this chapter has suggested a number of recommendations for practitioners working with parents, to support and encourage shared reading activity in the home. These, we hope, will help parents living in a variety of different contexts to develop and maintain enjoyable shared reading activities with their children. As we reflect back on the project, we are mindful of the fact that the children in this study were all of pre-school age. This does raise questions about the potential maintenance, or not, of shared reading activity in the home once children begin on the formal process of 'learning to read' in school. Of course, this was not investigated in the Shared Reading Project, however the findings do invite us to consider this question and the implications of this for practitioners working with families.

The final chapter of this book now looks towards the future. We consider the implications of the findings from this study for children as they start school and are confronted with a new definition of reading. We also consider the implications for parents and their shared reading activity in the home once their children start school.

10

SHARED READING AND STARTING SCHOOL – A CONCLUSION

This book has presented a strong argument for encouraging parents of young children to read regularly with their children, having shown how shared reading has numerous benefits for the child, parent and indeed the whole family unit. Many of the parents in the Shared Reading Project did enjoy strong reading relationships with their pre-school children, but this does lead us to wonder what may have happened once their children started school. Would these parents have continued to read with their children? We will never know the answer to this question as this was beyond the scope of the study, but what we do know is that most parents stop reading to their children by the time they are 8 years old (Nielsen Book Research, 2015). However, the project findings have compelled us to reflect on this question and consider the implications of this study for shared reading in families with school-age children. On the basis of findings drawn from the study, this chapter considers the role of the school discourse, suggesting that a dissonance between home and school may inhibit shared reading in the home. We then go on to compare the ways in which reading may be conceptualised within these two discourses, using this to argue that parents should be encouraged to read with their children way beyond their entry into the formal school system.

Shared reading and starting school

As authors, we began this book with an insight into our own interests in reading, with Rachael presenting an account of her own experiences of shared reading as a child, demonstrating how her interests in researching shared reading in the home had evolved from this. As we move into the conclusion we now present another story, again told in Rachael's words but in relation to another individual who we shall call Suzy. This story demonstrates why it is important to consider the school discourse in a book that is about shared reading in the home.

Suzy's story

Suzy is my hairdresser. I have known her for many years and in the spirit of many other hairdresser–client relationships, we have shared aspects of our daily lives and talked casually with one another about our jobs, families and daily activities, while my hair was being washed, cut and (with increasing regularity!) dyed. When, a few years ago, I learned that Suzy was expecting a baby, conversation naturally turned to baby-related topics. Several months later I was delighted to hear about the arrival of baby Josh, who remained a focus in our conversations for the years that followed. I enjoyed hearing about his first trip to the beach, his first words, and his boundless energy. Throughout these years, Suzy also told me how much she enjoyed reading with Josh and how receptive he was to being read to.

As Josh approached his fifth birthday, Suzy spoke with enthusiasm about the school that Josh would be going to, clearly excited about this new and important chapter in her son's life. But when I next saw Suzy it was clear that all was not well. Josh was not enjoying school and this was distressing for Suzy. She explained that much of the problem seemed to stem from the reading instruction that was taking place in school, as this appeared to cause particular tension in the classroom and particular misery for Josh. Josh was clearly becoming increasingly disengaged from reading and from school in general and this was causing Suzy considerable distress.

As we talked about Josh and the issues he was experiencing at school, I suggested to Suzy that she tried not to focus too much on the reading scheme books that were coming home each night, but rather just carry on reading their own books together. Suzy then told me that she had tried to do this, but Josh no longer wanted to be read to. She explained that Josh now appeared to have been put off books altogether. Suzy went on to tell me that she was really sad about this, because both she and Josh used to really enjoy sharing books together.

What we are seeing from Suzy's story is an example of a child who enjoyed shared reading in the home but became disengaged with reading once he started school. For Josh the construct of 'reading' had moved from the pleasurable activity of sharing books with his mother and listening to stories, to the act of decoding print within selected school books. Suzy's story suggests that Josh did not feel as if he was successful in this and as a result became unhappy with reading activity in school and disengaged from school altogether. What is more, Josh's resistance to reading in school seemed to filter into the home, which resulted in him rejecting contact with books even within the context of shared reading with his mother.

This illustrates how influential the school discourse can be as children develop perceptions of themselves as readers, and develop relationships with reading. We touched upon this issue in the second chapter of this book, in relation to one of the author's (Rachael's) previous research, which sought to understand children's perceptions of themselves as readers at the time of entry into the formal education system (Levy, 2011). Having studied two cohorts of young children over the course of an academic year, the study demonstrated that despite owning broad and inclusive definitions of reading while in Nursery (a pre-school year for children aged 3–4 years), these children quickly came to believe that reading was the decoding of print in books once they reached Reception (the first year of compulsory schooling for children aged 4–5 years).

Regardless of their perception of their own ability in reading, most of the children in this study seemed to think that being 'a reader' meant being able to decode print in reading scheme books. This connected with the fact that the children in this study seemed to believe that the reading scheme was responsible for *teaching* them how to read. This meant that the children thought that reading scheme books had to be rigorously and accurately decoded. For example, one child reported that she had 'to read every word' in a reading scheme book, clarifying that while it was acceptable to 'make up' the odd word in a storybook, she must not do this in a reading scheme book (Levy, 2009a). The children in this study had clearly come to believe that the reading scheme taught them how to read, but this meant that they also believed that until they had reached the point of completing the scheme, they were in fact unable to read.

This has serious implications for children's perceptions of themselves as readers, as this study suggested that children who are not progressing quickly through the reading scheme may be at risk of perceiving themselves as unsuccessful in reading or even being a non-reader. Given that these perceptions can become manifest from children's earliest days in school, and can be enduring, this is a serious issue. This is not to suggest that schools do not use reading schemes at all – indeed, reading scheme texts can play an important role in the process of teaching reading – rather this is highlighting that tools such as reading schemes should not be allowed to define a child's perception of themselves as a reader.

While the stringent use of a reading scheme seemed to be particularly influential in children's developing perceptions of themselves as readers, in the study discussed above, there has been a considerable amount written about the role of phonics more generally within the process of early reading. For example, Perkins and Goodwin, in a chapter by Macnair, Evans, Perkins and

Goodwin (2006: 54), argued that an explanation of what phonics is sounds 'surprisingly simple', before going on to state, 'yet it causes more debate among teachers, academics and politicians than any other aspect of the reading curriculum'. This seems to be largely connected to concerns about the ways in which aspects of phonics teaching can dominate how reading is perceived and defined as well as the implications of this for children's engagement with reading and confidence in themselves as readers.

A recent example of this is in relation to the Phonics Screening Check (DfE, 2012), which was administered for the first time in 2012 following a pilot in 2011. It is a statutory assessment for all Year 1 pupils in state schools in England. The purpose of the test is to ensure that children are able to decode using phonetic strategies. To make sure that children are in fact using phonics (and not just sight-reading), about half of the words in the test are 'pseudo words' (sometimes called 'nonsense words' or 'alien words'), which are made up of the phonemes and graphemes that a child has been taught, but are not real words. Examples of pseudo words are 'zorps', 'scroy' and 'gair'. But this raises serious questions about the message that schools are promoting in relation to what reading actually is, given that children are not only being asked to read words that are not real, but are being assessed on their ability to do this with accuracy. What is more, research into the impact of the Phonics Screening Check has revealed that the test has led to an increase in the amount and pace of phonics teaching and a greater focus on the use of decoding pseudo words (NFER, 2015), as well as a reduction in time being spent on whole-text activities (Hodgson & Buttle, 2013; UKLA, 2012).

Certainly some have suggested that the Phonics Screening Check may be directly responsible for some children losing confidence and motivation for reading (Hodgson & Buttle, 2013). It is not the role of this book to discuss phonics instruction, or indeed the teaching of reading in schools today, in any great detail, nevertheless there is good reason to raise concern about the impact of schooled definitions of reading, given that this differs substantially from the perspectives reported by the families in this book. If children are allowed to believe that reading *is* phonetic decoding, rather than seeing phonics as a strategy that will help them to access and enjoy texts for themselves, then it is easy to see how children and indeed some parents might come to view shared reading as less important, or even a distraction from the real business of teaching and learning to read.

In order to explore exactly why it is so important for parents to continue engaging in shared reading activity with their children once they start school, it is useful to return to the definition of shared reading that emerged from the Shared Reading Project, which was characterised by the Four T's. By comparing this home construction of shared reading with the ways in which reading is defined and presented within the school discourse, we quickly see that shared reading in the home provides children and their families with something that is not only different to school but is highly beneficial.

146

Reading at home and at school

As discussed in the previous chapter, through our conversations with the parents in our study, we were able to build a picture of what shared reading actually was for these families – we were able to understand what it looked like and how it operated. Having identified this as the Four T's, we now consider how each component (text, talk, time and togetherness) relates, or not, to schooled constructions of reading.

Text

We found that the parents in this study used texts in various ways to engage their children in meaningful literacy events. The text was focal to the activity in that it centred joint attention between parent and child, but the ways in which parents used texts was very flexible. Parents did read the words in books, but they were also comfortable in deviating from the print and would inject their own stories, songs and games into the activity. In brief, we found that the text often acted as a catalyst to facilitate communication between child and parent as well as encourage engagement in the activity in general.

This differs substantially from the ways in which texts, such as reading scheme books, are often used in the early years classroom. For the child starting school, many of the texts that they are faced with are books that come with the expectation that they must be rigorously decoded. These books are not there to facilitate conversation. The reader is not expected to deviate from the text, to add their own dialogue, to guess what words might say or miss out words or pages. These books need to be read sequentially and with accuracy. This reading is also linked with assessments and concepts of proficiency judgements.

This is not to suggest that teachers do not read to their children, indeed many do, but this is very often seen as an addition to the literacy curriculum rather than a vital component within it. Similarly, many early years classrooms are well stocked with picture books that children can access and, in many cases, even take home. But if a child has come to believe that 'real' reading is the decoding of print in reading scheme books, or the ability to read words on a worksheet, then this may have an impact on their engagement with texts outside of the reading scheme and/or outside of the school environment. This was clearly the case for Josh in Suzy's story.

Given that parents and teachers generally want children to engage confidently with a variety of texts, enjoy their interactions with text and have motivation for reading, then it underlines the importance of maintaining shared reading in the home after a child starts school. Of course, children must be taught how to decode print and indeed many children enjoy the process and enjoy the fact that they are progressing with this skill. But it is really important that children understand that this is a skill that will help them to read – rather than come to believe that this *is* reading. By continuing to enjoy the joint interactions with text that characterise shared reading between parent and child, children will be encouraged to recognise the various ways in which reading happens and value them as part of their everyday lives.

Talk

One of the crucial and defining features of shared reading was that it encouraged talk. The data in the project showed that the talk may have been centred on the text; however, parents also reported that shared reading also provided a space for parent and child to simply have time to talk about the day or anything else that was happening in their lives. Crucially, this talk was valued and was regarded by many as an important part of the shared reading experience.

This again differs from school in a number of ways. Firstly, when a child is being asked to read to an adult in school, the expectation is that the focus will be on the task of decoding the print. While children's talk is not always discouraged as such, limitations on time and resources and a concern for meeting statutory targets, generally means that the focus will be on the reading rather than the talking. What is more, the primary school classroom is not always a place where children's talk is valued. This was evidenced in a study conducted by Charlotte Wilders who studied six 6-year-old children in order to understand the impact of transition from an early childhood education setting to the first year of primary school, in a European school in Belgium (Wilders & Levy, 2020: 7–8). Wilders found that rules and rewards within the primary classroom were particularly contentious for these children, and this was especially clear in relation to rewards for 'working quietly' in the classroom. The children reported that the teacher would give a sticker to tables of children who were working quietly, with one boy clarifying 'when you're like chatting a lot she (teacher) doesn't give you a sticker'. For one child in the study, Katie, this was particularly problematic as she described herself as 'shy' and was working hard to communicate more freely with others. Consequently, the conflicting demands of trying to speak more, while also attempting to earn group rewards for 'being quiet' caused considerable tension for her. As a result, Katie ended up concluding that 'stickers annoy me sometimes', which was not surprising given that what Katie really needed was to be supported in talking more, rather than rewarded for being quiet.

Again we want to be clear that we are not suggesting that every class-room discourages children from talking – and we do appreciate that there is a need for quiet moments in the school day – but this does show how important shared reading in the home is, as it provides an opportunity to encourage children's talk after they start school. This is important in terms of language development but also, as many of the parents in the Shared Reading Project voiced, it provides an important opportunity for parents to bond with their child, understand how they are feeling and generally engage in daily communication.

Time

Linked with talk, many of the parents in this study told us that they valued the time that shared reading provided for them to spend with their children. As we have already discussed, shared reading seemed to offer parents a slice of protected time to spend with their child that may not otherwise have happened. As children start school, it may become even more difficult for parents to find time to spend with their child alone, especially if they have several children. This suggests that shared reading can support parents in finding time to spend with their children, given that the inclusion of regular shared reading activity can help to solidify routines into the day, which can ensure that parent and child have some time to spend together each day.

What is more, on the subject of time, even though many early years teachers try to ensure that they 'listen' to individual children reading at various points during the week, this is not the same as regularly sharing a whole text with a child on an individual basis. This rarely happens in classroom environments – there simply is not enough time. This again highlights how important it is for parents to continue spending time with their children, enjoying sharing a text together in a context that is free from the proficiency judgement that can emerge from the reading curriculum in schools.

Togetherness

Shared reading provided an opportunity for parent and child to bond and enjoy being together. As discussed in the previous chapter, the joint focus on a text often resulted in parent and child being physically close together, which roused the senses and encouraged closeness. Parents in the study greatly valued this and cherished the opportunity to connect with their child in this way.

The concept of closeness is not something that has been discussed in much detail in relation to primary school education. Physical closeness is not especially encouraged within the formal education system. What is more, as we write this concluding chapter, we are in the midst of particular unrest with regard to the notion of physical closeness due to the Covid-19 crisis. Anyone who has lived through the events of the Covid crisis will be aware of terms such as 'social distancing', 'bubble' and 'remote', all of which describe the current drive to keep individuals physically distanced from one another as far as possible, so as to prevent the spread of the Covid-19 virus. 'Lockdown' has seen children across the world being kept at a distance from their schools, but as children now return to their classrooms we are aware that the quest to keep distance from others is penetrating every aspect of children's education.

For example, there is debate about the wearing of face coverings, seating arrangements in the classroom, the size of groups, play-time arrangements and how teachers can interact with children. At the time of writing, we do not know with any certainty what the next few years will bring in relation to the Covid crisis, but what we do know is that we can expect a 'new normal' to persist for some time to come.

It seems very likely that for the foreseeable future, the notion of physical closeness and personal contact is something that will be discouraged in schools as well as in other aspects of children's lives outside of the home. Yet close contact is a human need and is a necessary factor in a child's emotional and physical development. Shared reading provides an opportunity for this closeness to happen. This again supports the assertion that parents should be encouraged to continue reading with their children for as long as they can.

Conclusion

This book has drawn on interviews with 29 parents in order to understand how shared reading operates within the everyday lives of families. We have shown how parents read with their children, what motivates them and what they need to sustain shared reading activity. We have also seen how important shared reading can be for the whole family, including establishing everyday routines, displaying constructs of 'being a family' and even supporting some parents' own relationships with reading. But above all we have seen how important shared reading can be for children.

This is the reason why we feel it is vital that practitioners from across disciplines, including, but not limited to those working in education, are able to encourage and support parents in reading with their children. Our conversations with parents has shown that shared reading works. It therefore seems appropriate that we close with some of the words from one of our participants (Lisa) who summarises many of the sentiments expressed in this book:

> To be honest it's quite relaxing, to just go up to her room with her and read a book. Yes – reading – yes. I love reading with her, mainly because I know she enjoys it .... that's why I like reading with her. I think it's just made her talk quicker, things like that, like her communication skills and stuff. I think it's very important to read and carry on reading.... So, I'll carry on reading with her until she asks me not to. Just seeing her enjoying it and seeing how much her talking and her writing and things like that are coming on. And do you know what I think? I think that's all down to reading...

REFERENCES

Aikens, N.L. and Barbarin, O. (2008). Socioeconomic differences in reading trajectories: The contribution of family, neighborhood, and school contexts. *Journal of Educational Psychology* 100(2): 235–251.

Albers, P., Frederick, T. and Cowan, K. (2009). Features of gender: An analysis of the visual texts of third grade children. *Journal of Early Childhood Literacy* 9(2): 234–260.

Alexander, S.T. (2013) Children of the book: Parents, bedtime and Jewish identity. *Journal of Jewish Education* 79(3): 174–198.

Aligagas, C. and Margallo, A.M. (2016). Children's responses to the interactivity of storybook apps in family shared reading events involving the iPad. *Literacy* 51(1): 44–52.

Alvermann, D.E. (2001). Reading adolescents' reading identities: Looking back to see ahead. *Journal of Adolescent & Adult Literacy* 44(8): 676–690.

Andrews, M., Squire, C. and Tamboukou, M. (Eds.) (2013). *Doing narrative research*. London: Sage.

Aram, D. and Biron, S. (2004). Joint storybook reading and joint writing interventions among low SES preschoolers: Differential contributions to early literacy. *Early Childhood Research Quarterly* 19: 588–610.

Aram, D. and Levin, I. (2002). Mother–child joint writing and storybook reading: Relations with literacy among low SES kindergartners. *Merrill-Palmer Quarterly* 48: 202–224.

Audet, D., Evans, M.A., Williamson, K. and Reynolds, K. (2008). Shared book reading: parental goals across the primary grades and goal–behaviour relationships in junior kindergarten. *Early Education and Development* 19(1): 112–137.

Aveling, N. (2002). 'Having it all' and the discourse of equal opportunity: Reflections on choices and changing perceptions. *Gender and Education* 14(3): 265–280.

Baker, L. (1999). Opportunities and home and in the community that foster reading engagement. In J.T. Guthrie and D.E. Alvermann (Eds.), *Engaged reading: Processes, practices, and policy implications* (pp. 105–133). New York: Teachers College, Columbia University.

Baker, L. and Scher, D. (2002). Beginning readers' motivation for reading in relation to parental beliefs and home reading experiences. *Reading Psychology* 23: 239–269.

Baker, L., Mackler, K., Sonnenschein, S. and Serpell, R. (2001). Parents' interactions with their first-grade children during storybook reading and relations with subsequent home reading activity and reading achievement. *Journal of School Psychology* 39: 415–438.

Baker, L., Scher, D. and Mackler, K. (1997). Home and family influences on motivations for reading. *Educational Psychologist* 32(2): 69–82.

Baker, L., Serpell, R. and Sonnenschein, S. (1995). Opportunities for literacy learning in the homes of urban preschoolers. In L.M. Morrow (Ed.), *Family literacy: Connections in schools and communities* (pp. 236–252). Newark, DE: International Reading Association.

Baldwin, D. and Moses, L. (1996). The ontogeny of social information gathering. *Child Development* 67: 1915–1939.

Barton, D. (2007). *Literacy: An introduction to the ecology of written language.* Oxford: Blackwell.

Bathmaker, A.M. and Harnett, P. (Eds.) (2010). *Exploring learning, identity and power through life history and narrative research.* London: Routledge.

Bearne, E. (2003). Rethinking literacy: Communication, representation and text. *Reading* 37(3): 98–103.

Bergin, C. (2001). The parent–child relationship during beginning reading. *Journal of Literacy Research* 33: 681–706.

Bingham, G.E. (2007). Maternal literacy beliefs and the quality of mother-child book-reading interactions: Associations with children's early literacy development. *Early Education and Development* 18: 23–49.

Boardman, K. (2019). The incongruities of 'teaching phonics' with two-year olds, *Education 3–13*, 47(7): 842–853.

Bourdieu, P. (1992). *The logic of practice.* Cambridge: Polity.

Braun, V. and Clarke, V. (2006). Using thematic analysis in psychology. *Qualitative Research in Psychology* 3(2): 77–101.

Braun, V. and Clarke, V. (2013). *Successful qualitative research: A practical guide for beginners.* London: Sage.

Britto, P.R., Brooks-Gunn, J. and Griffin, T.M. (2006). Maternal reading and teaching patterns: Associations with school readiness in low-income African American families. *Reading Research Quarterly* 41: 68–89. doi:10.1598/RRQ.41.1.3

Britto, P.R., Fuligni, A.S. and Brooks-Gunn, J. (2002). Reading, rhymes and routines: American parents and their young children. In N. Halfon, K. Taaffe McClearn and M.A. Schuster, (Eds.), *Child rearing in America.* Cambridge: Cambridge University Press.

Bronfenbrenner, U. (1979). *The ecology of human development: Experiments by nature and design.* Cambridge, MA: Harvard University Press.

Bronfenbrenner, U. (1986). Ecology of the family as a context for human development: Research perspectives. *Developmental Psychology* 22(6): 723–774.

Bronfenbrenner, U. (1990). Discovering what families do. In D. Balnkenhorn, S. Bayme and J.B. Elshtain (Eds.), *Rebuilding the nest: A new commitment to the American family* (pp. 27–38). Milwaukee, WI: Family Service America.

Brooker, L. (2002) *Starting school: Young children learning cultures,* Buckingham: Open University Press.

Brooks-Gunn, J., Klebanov, P. and Duncan, D. (1996). Ethnic differences in children's intelligence test scores: Role of economic deprivation, home environment, and maternal characteristics. *Child Development* 67: 396–408.

Brown, P.M., Byrnes, L.J., Watson, L.M. and Raban, B. (2013). Young learners: Aspects of home literacy environments supporting hypotheses about the structure of printed words. *Journal of Early Childhood Research* 11(3): 262–273.

Brunt, L. (2001). Into the community. In P. Atkinson, A. Coffey, S. Delamont, J. Lofland and L. Lofland (Eds.), *Handbook of ethnography* (pp. 80–91). London: Sage.

Bryman, A. (2016). *Social research methods.* Oxford: Oxford University Press.

Burgess, R.G. (1984). *In the field: An introduction to field research.* London: Unwin Hyman.

Burgess, S.R. (2002). The influence of speech perception, oral language ability, home literacy environment, and pre-reading knowledge on the growth of phonological sensitivity: A one-year longitudinal investigation. *Reading and Writing: An Interdisciplinary Journal* 15: 709–737.

Bus, A.G., Van Ijzendoorn, M. and Pellegrini, A.D. (1995) Joint book reading makes for success in learning to read: A meta-analysis on intergenerational transmission of literacy. *Review of Educational Research*, 65: 1–21.

Bus, A.G., Belsky, J., Van Ijzendoom, M.H. and Crnic, K. (1997). Attachment and bookreading patterns: A study of mothers, fathers, and their toddlers. *Early Childhood Research Quarterly* 12: 81–98.

Bus, A.G., de Jong, M.T. and Van Ijzendoorn, M.H. (2007). Social aspects in language and literacy learning: Progress, problems, and interventions. In O.N. Saracho and B. Spodek (Eds.), *Contemporary perspectives on social learning in early childhood education* (Vol. IX, pp. 243–257). Greenwich, CT: Information Age.

Bynner, J. and Parsons, S. (2006). *New light on literacy and numeracy.* London: NRDC.

Carr, W. and Harnett, A. (1996). *Education and the struggle for democracy. democratic theory and democratic education.* Buckingham: Open University Press.

Carrington, V. and Robinson, M. (2009). *Digital literacies: social learning and classroom practices.* London: Sage.

Clark, C. and Hawkins, L. (2010). Young people's reading: The importance of the home environment and family support. More findings from our national survey. National Literacy Trust.

Clark, C. and Rumbold, K. (2006). Reading for pleasure: A research overview. National Literacy Trust.

Clark, C. and Teravainen, A. (2017) What it means to be a reader at age 11: valuing skills, affective components and behavioural processes. The National Literacy Trust.

Cole, M. (1996). *Cultural psychology: A once and future discipline.* Cambridge, MA: Harvard University Press.

Cove, M. (2006). Sounds familiar: The history of phonics teaching. In M. Lewis and S. Ellis, (Eds,), *Phonics: Practice research and policy.* London: Sage.

Curtis, P., James, A. and Ellis, K. (2010). Children's snacking, children's food: food moralities and family life. *Children's Geographies* 8(3): 291–302.

David, A. (2014). *Help your child love reading: a parents guide.* London: Egmont.

Davies, K. and Mason, J. (2008). Findings leaflet: Living Resemblances project. http://eprints.ncrm.ac.uk/1115/1/resemblances-project-leaflet.pdf

DeBaryshe, B.D. (1995). Maternal belief systems: Linchpin in the home reading process. *Journal of Applied Developmental Psychology*, 16: 1–20.

DeBaryshe, B.D., Binder, J.C. and Buell, M.B. (2000) Mothers' implicit theories of early literacy instruction: implications for children's reading and writing. *Early Child Development and Care*, 160(1): 119–131.

de Jong, M., Mol, S. and Bus, A. (2009). Home literacy environment and literacy outcomes from childhood throughout young adulthood: A meta-analysis on the effects of print exposure. Presentation at the 16th Annual Meeting of the Society for the Scientific Study of Reading, June, Boston, MA.

Denney, M.K., Moore, K. and Snyder, P. (2010). *Supporting parent and caregiver involvement in early literacy practices with young children from diverse backgrounds and abilities*. Washington, DC: Head Start Center for Inclusion.

Denzin, N.K. [1977] (2017). *Childhood socialization*. Oxon: Routledge.

Denzin, N.K. (1989). *Interpretive interactionism*. Newbury Park, CA: Sage.

DFE (2012). Phonics screening check and key stage 1 assessments: England 2012. DfE.

DfES (2005). *Independent review of the teaching of early reading: Interim report to DfES*. London: DfES.

DfES (2006). *Independent review of the teaching of early reading (The Rose Review)*. London: DfES

Dickinson, D.K. (2001). Book reading in preschool classrooms: Is recommended practice common? In D.K. Dickinson and P.O. Tabors (Eds.), *Beginning literacy with language: Young children learning at home and school* (pp. 175–203). Baltimore, MD: Brookes.

Douglas, J.W.B. (1964). *The home and the school* (p. 98). London: MacGibbon & Kee.

Duncan, G., Brooks-Gunn, J. and Klebanov, P. (1994). Economic deprivation and early child development. *Child Development* 65: 296–318.

Edwards, R. and Gillies, V. (2012). Farewell to family? Notes on an argument for retaining the concept. *Families, Relationships and Societies* 1(1): 63–69.

Egmont (2013). *Reading street* (ch.1–3). Available at: https://www.egmont.co.uk/reading-fun/reading-street/

Eliot, L. (2009). *Pink brain, blue brain*. Oxford: Oneworld.

Ellis, J., (2013). Thinking beyond rupture: continuity and relationality in everyday illness and dying experience. *Mortality* 18(3): 251–269.

Epstein, J., Jansom, N.R., Sheldon, S.B. and Sanders, M.G. (2008). *School, family and community partnerships: Your handbook for action*. Thousand Oaks, CA: Corwin Press.

Erikson, E.H. (1968). *Identity: Youth and crisis*. New York: Norton.

Fiese, B.H. (2002). Routines of daily living and rituals in family life: A glimpse at stability and change during the early child-raising years. *Zero to Three* 22: 10–13.

Fiese, B.H. (2006). *Family routines and rituals*. New Haven, CT: Yale University Press.

Fiese, B.H. and Everhart, R.S. (2008). Routines and child development. In M. Haith and J. Benson (Eds.), *Encyclopedia of infant and early childhood development* (pp. 34–41). San Diego, CA: Academic Press.

Finch, J. (2007). Displaying families. *Sociology* 41(1): 65–81.

Fine, C. (2010). *Delusions of gender*. London: Icon Books.

Fletcher, K.L. and Reese, E. (2005). Picture book reading with young children: A conceptual framework. *Developmental Review* 25(1): 64–103.

Fraser, H. (2004). Doing narrative research: Analysing personal stories line by line. *Qualitative Social Work* 3(2): 179–201.

Frijters, J.C., Barron, R.W. and Brunello, M. (2000). Direct and mediated influences of home literacy and literacy interest on prereaders' oral vocabulary and early written language skill. *Journal of Educational Psychology* 92: 466–477.

Frosch, C.A., Cox, M.J. and Goldman, B.D. (2001). Infant–parent attachment and parental and child behaviour during parent toddler storybook interaction. *Merrill-Palmer Quarterly* 47(4): 445–474.

Gabb, J., (2008). *Researching intimacy in families.* Basingstoke: Palgrave Macmillan.

Galbraith, G. (1997). *Reading Lives; Reconstructing childhood, books, and schools in Britain, 1870–1920.* London: Macmillan.

Gammage, P. (2006). Early childhood education and care: politics, policies and possibilities. *Early Years* 26(3): 235–248.

Gauvain, M. (2005) Sociocultural contexts of learning. In A.E. Maynard and M.I. Martini, (Eds.), *Learning in cultural context, family, peers and school.* Dordrecht: Kluwer Academic / Plenum Publishers.

Gergen, K.J. (2009). *Relational being: Beyond self and community.* New York: Oxford University Press.

Gillies, V. (2010). Is poor parenting a class issue? Contextualising anti-social behaviour and family life. In M. Klett-Davies (Eds.), *Is parenting a class issue?* (pp 44–61). London: Family and Parenting Institute.

Gjems, L. (2010). Teachers talking to young children: invitations to negotiate meaning in everyday conversations. *European Early Childhood Education Research Journal* 18(2): 139–148.

Goodson, I., Antikainen, A., Sikes, P. and Andrews, M. (Eds.). (2016). *The Routledge international handbook on narrative and life history.* New York: Taylor & Francis.

Goodwin, M. (1990). *He-said-she-said: Talk as social organisation amongst black children.* Bloomington, IN: Indiana University Press.

Gopnik, A., Meltzoff, A.N. and Kuhl, P.K. (1999). *The scientist in the crib: Minds, brains, and how children learn.* New York: William Morrow & Co.

Graff, H.J. (1987). *The labyrinths of literacy: Reflections on literacy past and present.* Oxon: Falmer Press.

Greenleaf, C.L. and Hinchman, K. (2009). Reimagining our inexperienced adolescent readers: From struggling, striving, marginalized, and reluctant to thriving. *Journal of Adolescent & Adult Literacy* 53(1): 4–13.

Gregory, E. and Ruby, M. (2011). The 'insider/outsider'dilemma of ethnography: Working with young children and their families in cross-cultural contexts. *Journal of Early Childhood Research* 9(2): 162–174.

Grieshaber, S., Shield, P., Luke, A. and Macdonald, S. (2012). Family literacy practices and home literacy resources: An Australian pilot study. *Journal of Early Childhood Literacy* 12(2): 113–138.

Griffin, E.A. and Morrison, F.J. (1997) The unique contribution of home literacy environment to differences in early literacy skills. *Early Child Development and Care* 127(1): 233–243.

Guthrie, J.T. and Wigfield, A. (2000). Engagement and motivation in reading. In M.L. Kamil, P.B. Mosenthal, P.D. Pearson and R. Barr (Eds.), *Handbook of reading research* (Vol III, pp. 403–422). New York: Erlbaum.

Gutierrez, K. and Stone, L. (1997). A cultural-historical view of learning and learning disabilities: participating in a community of learners. *Learning Disabilities Research and Practice* 12(2): 123–131.

Hale, L., Berger, L.M., LeBourgeois, M.K. and Brooks-Gunn, J. (2009). Social and demographic predictors of preschoolers' bedtime routines. *Journal of Developmental and Behavioral Pediatrics* 30: 394–402.

Hale, L., Berger, L.M., LeBourgeois, M.K. and Brooks-Gunn, J. (2011). A longitudinal study of preschoolers. *Journal of Family Psychology* 25: 423.

Hall, K. (2006) How children learn to read and how phonics helps. In M. Lewis, and S. Ellis, (Eds,), *Phonics: Practice research and policy*. London: Sage.

Hall, M. and Sikes, P. (2018). How do young people 'do' family where there is a diagnosis of dementia?. *Families, Relationships and Societies* 7(2): 207–225.

Hardman, M. and Jones, L. (1999) Sharing books with babies: Evaluation of an early literacy intervention. *Educational Review* 51: 220–229.

Harman, V. and Cappellini, B. (2015). Mothers on display: Lunchboxes, social class and moral accountability. *Sociology* 49(4): 764–781.

Harris, A., Andrew-Power, K. and Goodall, J. (2009) *Do parents know they matter? Raising achievement through parental engagement*. London: Continuum.

Harris, K.K., Loyo, J., Holahan, C., et al. (2007). Cross-sectional predictors of reading to young children among participants in the Texas WIC program. *Journal of Research in Childhood Education* 21: 254–268.

Havelock, E. (1976). *Origins of Western literacy*. Toronto: Ontario Institute for Studies in Education.

Heath, S.B. (1982). What no bedtime story means: Narrative skills at home and at school. *Language in Society*, 11(1): 49–76.

Heath, S.B. (1983). *Ways with words: Language, life and work in communities and classrooms*. Cambridge: Cambridge University Press.

Henderson, A.T., Mapp, K. and Johnson, V.R. (2007). *Beyond the bake sale: The essential guide to family-school partnerships*, New York: The New Press.

Hewison, J. and Tizard, J. (1980). Parental involvement and reading attainment. *British Journal of Educational Psychology* 50: 209–215.

Hindman, A.H., Connor, C.M., Jewkes, A.M. and Morrison, F.J. (2008). Untangling the effects of shared book reading: Multiple factors and their associations with preschool literacy outcomes. *Early Childhood Research Quarterly* 23: 330–350.

Hodgson, J., Buttle, H., Conridge, B., Gibbons, D. and Robinson, J. (NATE) (2013). Phonics instruction and early reading: professional views from the classroom. Accessed from www.nate.org.uk.

Holloway, S.L. and Pimlott-Wilson, H. (2014) 'Any advice is welcome isn't it?': Neoliberal parenting education, local mothering cultures, and social class. *Environment and Planning A* 46(1): 94–111.

Hutcheon, L. (2012). *A theory of adaptation*. London: Routledge.

James, A. (2013). *Socialising children*. Basingstoke: Palgrave Macmillan.

James, C. (2009). *Ten years of family policy: 1999–2009*. London: Family and Parenting Institute .

James, A. and Curtis, P. (2010). Family displays and personal lives. *Sociology* 44(6): 1163–1180.

Jamieson, L., Lewis, R. and Simpson, R. (2011). *Researching families and relationships: Reflections on process*. London: Palgrave.

Jardine, C. (2017). Constructing and maintaining family in the context of imprisonment. *The British Journal of Criminology* 58(1): 114–131.

Josselson, R. and Lieblich, A. (1999). *Making meaning of narratives* (6th ed.). London: Sage.

Justice, L.M., Logan, J.R. and Damschroder, L. (2015). Designing caregiver-implemented shared-reading interventions to overcome implementation barriers. *Journal of Speech and Language and Hearing Research* 58(6): 1851–1863. doi:10.1044/2015_JSLHR-L14-0344

Justice, L.M., Skibbe, L.E., McGinty, A.S., Piasta, S.B. and Petrill, S. (2011). Feasibility, efficacy, and social validity of home-based storybook reading intervention for children with language impairment. *Journal of Speech, Language, and Hearing Research* 54(2): 523–538

Karrass, J., Braungart-Rieker, J.M., Mullins, J. and Lefever, J.B. (2002). Processes in language acquisition: The roles of gender, attention, and maternal encouragement of attention over time. *Journal of Child Language* 29: 519–543.

Kelly, J.N., Jarrett, R.L. and Williams-Wheeler, M. (2016). 'We pray, and we read… ..I let them watch some TV': African American preschoolers' bedtime experiences with literacy. *The Western Journal of Black Studies* 40(3): 174–191.

Klett-Davies M. (Ed.) (2010). *Is parenting a class issue?* London: Family and Parenting Institute.

Kress, G. (2003). *Literacy in the new media age.* London: Routledge.

Kucirkova, N., Dale, P.S. and Sylva K. (2018). Parents reading with their 10-month-old babies: key predictors for high-quality reading styles. *Early Child Development and Care.* 188(2): 195–207

Leseman, P.P.M. and de Jong, P.F. (1998). Home literacy: Opportunity, instruction, cooperation, and social-emotional quality predicting early reading achievement. *Reading Research Quarterly* 33: 294–318. doi: 10.1598/RRQ.33.3.3

Levy, R. (2008). Third spaces' are interesting places; applying 'third space theory' to nursery-aged children's constructions of themselves as readers. *Journal of Early Childhood Literacy* 8(1): 43–66.

Levy, R. (2009a). Children's perceptions of reading and the use of reading scheme texts. *Cambridge Journal of Education* 39(3): 361–377.

Levy, R. (2009b). 'You have to understand words … but not read them'; young children becoming readers in a digital age. *Journal of Research in Reading* 32(1): 75–91.

Levy, R. (2011). *Young children reading at home and at school,* London: Sage.

Levy, R. (2016). A historical reflection on literacy, gender and opportunity: implications for the teaching of literacy in early childhood education. *International Journal of Early Years Education* 24(3): 279–293.

Levy, R. and Marsh, J. (2011). Literacy and ICT in the early years. In D. Lapp and D. Fisher (Eds.), *The handbook of research on teaching the English language arts* (3rd ed.). Mahwah, NJ: Lawrence Erlbaum Associates.

Levy, R., Little, S., Clough, P., Nutbrown, C., Bishop, J., Lamb, T. and Yamada-Rice, D. (2014). *Attitudes to Reading and Writing and their Links with Social Mobility 1914–2014: An Evidence Review, for Booktrust.*

Lewis, M. and Ellis, S. (2006). Phonics: The wider picture. In M. Lewis and S. Ellis (Eds.), *Phonics: practice, research and policy.* London: Sage.

Lin, J., Stephanie, M.R., Sabrina, K., et al. (2015). Maternal reading self-efficacy associated with perceived barriers to reading. *Child Development Research* 2015: 1–7.

Logan, S., Medford, E. and Hughes, N. (2011), The importance of intrinsic motivation for high and low ability readers' reading comprehension performance. *Learning and Individual Differences* 21: 124–128.

Luke, A. (1996). Genres of power? In R. Hasan and G. Williams (Eds.), *Literacy in power*. London: Longmans.

Macnair, L., Evans, S., Perkins, M. and Goodwin, P. (2006). Inside the classroom: Approaches to phonics teaching. In M. Lewis and S. Ellis (Eds.), *Phonics: Practice research and policy*. London: Sage.

Mangen, A. and van der Weel, A. (2016) The evolution of reading in the age of digitisation: an integrative framework for reading research. *Literacy* 50(3): 116–124.

Mansell, J., Evans, M.A. and Hamilton-Hulak, L. (2005). Developmental changes in parents' use of miscue feedback during shared book reading. *Reading Research Quarterly* 40: 294–317.

Marsh, J. (2005). Children of the digital age. In J. Marsh (Ed.), *Popular culture, new media and digital literacy in early childhood* (pp.1–10). London: RoutledgeFalmer.

Marsh, J. and Singleton, C. (2009) Editorial: Literacy and technology: questions of relationship. *Journal of Research in Reading* 32(1): 1–5.

Marsh, J., Brookes, G., Hughes, J., Ritchie, L, Roberts, S. and Wright, K. (2005). *Digital beginnings: Young children's use of popular culture, media and new technologies*. Literacy Research Centre, University of Sheffield.

Martens, L. (2012). Practice 'in talk'and talk 'as practice': Dish washing and the reach of language. *Sociological Research Online* 17(3): 1–11.

Martin-Chang, S. and Gould, O.N. (2012). Reading to children and listening to children read: Mother–child interactions as a function of principal reader. *Early Education & Development* 23(6): 855–876.

Mason, J. (2008). Tangible affinities and the real life fascination of kinship. *Sociology* 42(1): 29–45.

Mason, J. (2018). *Affinities: Potent connections in personal life*. New York: Wiley.

Mauthner, M., Birch, M., Jessop, J. and Miller, T. (Eds.) (2002). *Ethics in qualitative research*. London: Sage.

McCabe, A. and Bliss, L.S. (2003). *Patterns of narrative discourse: A multicultural, life span approach*. London: Allyn & Bacon.

McGuinness, D. (2005). *Language development and learning to read*. London: MIT Press.

McKeown, K. (2001). *Fathers and families: research and reflection on key questions*. Social and Economic Research Consultants.

McNamara, O., Hustler, D., Stronach, I., Rodrigo, M., Beresford, E. and Botcherby, S. (2000). Room to manoeuvre: Mobilising the „active partner" in home-school relations. *British Educational Research Journal* 26(4): 473–489.

Medford, E. and McGeown, S. (2011). Cognitive and motivational factors for reading: The need for a domain specific approach to motivation. In J. Franco and A. Svensgaard (Eds.), *Psychology of motivation: New research*. New York: Nova Science Publications.

Mehan, H. (1996). The construction of an LD student: a case study in the politics of representation. In M. Silverstein and G. Urban (Eds.), *Natural histories of discourse* (pp. 253–276). Chicago, IL: University of Chicago Press.

Merchant, G. (2007). Writing in the future in the digital age. *Literacy* 41(3): 118–128.

Merchant, G. (2015). Keep taking the tablets: iPads, story apps and early literacy. *Australian Journal of Language and Literacy* 38(1): 3–11.

Meskin, A. (2011). The philosophy of comics. *Philosophy Compass* 6(12): 854–864.

Milan, S., Snow, S. and Belay, S. (2007) The context of preschool children's sleep: Racial/ethnic differences in sleep locations, routines, and concerns. *Journal of Family Psychology*, 21: 20–28.

Mindell, J.A. and Williamson, A.A. (2018). Benefits of a bedtime routine in young children: Sleep, development, and beyond. *Sleep Medicine Reviews* 40: 93–108.

Mindell, J.A., Meltzer, L.J., Carskadon, M.A. and Chervin, R.D. (2009). Developmental aspects of sleep hygiene: Findings from the 2004 National Sleep Foundation Sleep in America poll. *Sleep Medicine* 10: 771–779.

Minns, H. (1990). *Read it to me now; learning at home and at school.* London: Virago Press.

Mol, S.E., Bus, A.G., de Jong, M.T. and Smeets, D. (2008). Added value of dialogic parent–child book readings: A meta-analysis. *Early Education & Development* 19: 7–26.

Morgan, A., Nutbrown, C. and Hannon, P. (2009). Fathers' involvement in young children's literacy development: implications for family literacy programmes. *British Educational Research Journal* 35(2): 167–185.

Morgan, D. (2011). *Rethinking family practices.* Berlin: Springer.

Morgan, D. (2018). *Snobbery: The practices of distinction.* Bristol: Policy Press.

Morgan, D.H. (1996). *Family connections: An introduction to family studies.* Cambridge: Polity Press.

Morris, D. and Jones, K. (2007). Minority language socialisation within the family: Investigating the early welsh language socialisation of babies and young children in mixed language families in Wales. *Journal of Multilingual and Multicultural Development*, 28(6): 484–501.

Moss, G. (2000). Raising boys' attainment in reading: Some principles for intervention. *Reading* 34(3): 101–106.

Mullan, K. (2010). Families that read: A time-diary analysis of young people's and parents' reading. *Journal of Research in Reading* 33(4): 414–430.

Mullis, I., Martin, M., Foy, P. and Drucker, K. (2011) PIRLS 2011 International Results in Reading, IEA.

Nichols, S. (2000). Unsettling the bedtime story: parents' reports of home literacy practices. *Contemporary Issues in Early Childhood Education*, 1(3): 315–328.

Nielsen Book Research (2015). Understanding the Children's and Young Adult Book Report, Neilson Book.

Nutbrown, C. and Page, J. (2008). *Working with babies and children: From birth to three.* London: Sage.

Oakley, A. (2013). Interviewing women: A contradiction in terms. *Doing feminist research* (pp. 52–83). London: Routledge.

OECD (2002). *Reading for change: Performance and engagement across countries.* Paris: Organisaiton for Economic Cooperation and Development.

Ouellette, J. (2010). *The calculus diaries: How math can help you lose weight, win in Vegas, and survive a zombie apocalypse.* London: Penguin.

Pahl, K. and Rowsell, J. (2010) *Artifactual literacies,* New York: Teachers College Press.

Papacharissi, Z. (2012). Kenneth J. Gergen, relational being: Beyond self and community. *International Journal of Communication* 6: 4.

Park, H. (2008). Home literacy environments and children's reading performance: A comparative study of 25 countries. *Educational Research and Evaluation* 14(6): 489–505.

Pew Research Center (2016). Book Reading 2016. Available at: http://www.pewinternet.org/files/2016/08/PI_2016.09.01_Book-Reading_FINAL.pdf

Phoenix, A. and Brannen, J. (2014). Researching family practices in everyday life: Methodological reflections from two studies. *International Journal of Social Research Methodology* 17(1): 11–26.

Plummer, K. (2001). *Documents of life 2: An invitation to a critical humanism* (Vol. 2). London: Sage.

Plummer, K. (2002). *Telling sexual stories: Power, change and social worlds.* London: Routledge.

Price, L.H., van Kleeck, A. and Huberty, C.J. (2009). Talk during book sharing between parents and preschool children: A comparison between storybook and expository book conditions. *Reading Research Quarterly* 44(2): 171–194.

Publishers Association (2015). *PA statistics yearbook.* London: The Publishers Association.

Ramsey-Kurz, H. (2007). *The non-literate other: Readings of illiteracy in twentieth-century novels in English.* Amsterdam: Rodopi.

Read On. Get On. (2017). What it means to be a reader at age 11 – valuing skills, affective and behavioural processes. Published by the National Literacy Trust on behalf of the Read On. Get On. Coalition. https://literacytrust.org.uk/policy-and-campaigns/read-on-get-on/

Reay, D. (1998). *Class work: Mothers' involvement in their children's primary schooling.* London: Routledge Falmer.

Reay, D. (2004). It's all becoming a habitus': Beyond the habitual use of habitus in educational research. *British Journal of Sociology of Education* 25(4): 431–444.

Reay, D. (2017). *Miseducation.* Bristol: Policy Press.

Reese, L. and Gallimore, R. (2000). Immigrant Latinos' cultural model of literacy development: An evolving perspective on home-school discontinuities. *American Journal of Education* 108(2): 103–134.

Reinharz, S. (1992). *Feminist methods in social research.* New York: Oxford University Press.

Ren, L. and Hu, G. (2011). A comparative study of family social capital and literacy practices in Singapore. *Journal of Early Childhood Literacy* 13(1): 98–130.

Riessman, C.K. (1993). *Narrative analysis* (Vol. 30). Sage: London.

Ross, K.M., Pye, R.E. and Randell, J. (2016). Reading touch screen storybooks with mothers negatively affects 7-year-old readers' comprehension but enriches emotional engagement. *Frontiers in Psychology* 7 (article 1728): 1–17.

Saracho, O.N. (2017). Parents' shared storybook reading; Learning to read. *Early Child Development and Care* 187(3–4): 554–567.

Savage, M. (2015). *Social class in the 21st century.* London: Pelican.

Sawyer, B.E., Cycyk, L.M., Sandilos, L.E. and Hammer, C.S. (2016) 'So many books they don't even all fit on the bookshelf': An examination of low-income mothers' home literacy practices, beliefs and influencing factors. *Journal of Early Childhood Literacy*, 18(3): 338–372.

Scher, D. and Baker, L. (1996, April). Attitudes toward reading and children's home literacy environments. Poster session presented at the meeting of the American Educational Research Association, New York.

Senechal, M. and LeFevre, J. (2001). Storybook reading and parent teaching: Links to language and literacy development. In P.R. Britto and J. Brooks-Gunn (Eds.), *The role of family literacy environments in promoting young children's emerging literacy skills* (pp. 39–52). San Francisco, CA: Jossey-Bass.

Senechal, M. and LeFevre, J.A. (2002). Parental involvement in the development of children's reading skill: A five-year longitudinal study. *Child Development* 73: 445–460.

Sénéchal, M. and Young, L. (2008). The effect of family literacy interventions on children's acquisition of reading from kindergarten to grade 3: A meta-analytic review. *Review of Educational Research* 78(4): 880–907.

Sénéchal, M., LeFevre, J.A., Hudson, E. and Lawson, P.E. (1996). Knowledge of storybooks as a predictor of young children's vocabulary. *Journal of Educational Psychology* 88: 520–536.

Shirani, F., Henwood, K. and Coltart, C. (2012). Meeting the challenges of intensive parenting culture: Gender, risk management and the moral parent. *Sociology* 46(1): 25–40.

Shove, E., Pantzar, M. and Watson, M. (2012). *The dynamics of social practice: Everyday life and how it changes*. London: Sage.

Sim, S. and Berthelsen, D. (2014). Shared book reading by parents with young children: evidence-based practice. *Australasian Journal of Early Childhood* 39(1): 50–55.

Skeggs, B. (1997). *Formations of class & gender: Becoming respectable* (Vol. 51). London: Sage.

Skinner, T. (2013). Women's perceptions of how their dyslexia impacts on their mothering. *Disability & Society* 28(1): 81–95.

Smart, C. (2007). *Personal life*. Cambridge: Polity.

Snow, C. (1994). Enhancing literacy development: programs and research perspectives. In D.K. Dickinson (Ed.), *Bridges to literacy*. Oxford: Blackwell.

SOEID (The Scottish Office Education and Industry Department) (1998). *Interchange 57 Accelerating Reading Attainment: The effectiveness of synthetic phonics*. Edinburgh: SOEID.

Sonnenschein, S., Brody, G. and Munsterman, K. (1996). The influence of family beliefs and practices on children's early reading development. In L. Baker, P. Afflerbach and D. Reinking (Eds.), *Developing engaged readers in school and home communities* (pp. 3–20). Hillsdale, NJ: Erlbaum.

Starkey, L. (2012). *Teaching and learning in the digital age*. London, Routledge.

Strathern, M. (2005). *Partial connections*. Altamira: Rowman.

Styles, M. (1997). 'Of the spontaneous kind?': Women writing poetry for children – from Jane Johnson to Christina Rosetti, in M. Hilton, M. Styles and V. Watson (Eds.), *Opening the nursery door* (pp.142–158). London: Routledge.

Swaffield, L. (2017). The UK no longer has a public library system. *The Guardian* 19 October 2017. Available at: https://www.theguardian.com/voluntary-sector-network/2017/oct/19/uk-national-public-library-system-community [Accessed 2 Jul. 2019].

Sylva, K., Melhuish, E., Sammons, P., Siraj-Blatchford, I. and Taggart, B. (2004). *The effective provision of pre-school education project: effective pre-school education.* Final Report Nottingham: DfES/London Institute of Education.

The Reader Organisation (accessed 27 March 2019). https://www.thereader.org.uk/about/wherewework/

Thomas, W.I. and Znaniecki, F. (1918). *The Polish peasant in Europe and America: Monograph of an immigrant group* (Vol. 2). Chicago: University of Chicago Press.

Thomson, R. and Kehily, M.J. (2011). *Making modern mothers.* Bristol: Policy Press.

Tizard, J., Schofield, W.N. and Hewison, J. (1982). Collaboration between teachers and parents in assisting children's reading. *British Journal of Educational Psychology* 52: 1–15.

UKLA (2012). UKLA Analysis of Schools' response to the Year 1 Phonics Screening Check, accessed from www.ukla.org.uk

Vanobbergen, B., Daems, M. and Tilburg, S. (2009). Bookbabies, their parents and the library: an evaluation of a Flemish reading programme in families with young children. *Educational Review* 61(3): 277–287.

Vincent, C. (2017). The children have only got one education and you have to make sure it's a good one': parenting and parent–school relations in a neoliberal age. *Gender and Education* 29(5): 541–557.

Walker, M., Bartlett, S., Betts, H., Sainsbury, M. and Worth, J. (NFER) (2015). Phonics screening check evaluation. DfE.

Walsh, M. (2011). Review of Pahl, K. and Rowsell, J. (2011). Artifactual literacies. *Journal of Early Childhood Literacy* 11(4): 501–503.

Weinberger, J. (1996). A longitudinal study of children's early literacy experiences at home and later literacy development at home and school. *Journal of Research in Reading* 19: 14–24.

Wengraf, T. (2001). *Qualitative research interviewing: Biographic narrative and semi-structured methods.* London: Sage.

Whalley, M. (2007). *Involving parents in their children's learning* (2nd ed.). Thousand Oaks, CA: Sage.

Wheater, R., Ager, R., Burge, B. and Sizmur, J. (2014). Achievement of 15-Year-Olds in England: PISA 2012 National Report (OECD Programme for International Student Assessment, DfE.

Wilders, C. and Levy, R. (2020). I don't really like the thing what you do, I like it more because you get the stickers: the impact of rules and rewards on children's transition experiences. *International Journal of Early Years Education.* Published online 12 May 2020.

Williams, F., (2004). *Rethinking families.* London: Calouste Gulbenkian Foundation.

Wolfendale, S. (1985). An introduction to parent listening. In K. Topping and S. Wolfendale (Eds.), *Parental involvement in children's reading.* London: Croom Helm,

Yu, C. and Smith, L.B. (2017). Hand-eye coordination predicts joint attention. *Child Development* 88(6): 2060–2078.

Yuill, N. and Martin, A.F. (2016). Curling up with a good e-book: Mother–child shared story reading on screen or paper affects embodied interaction and warmth. *Frontiers in Psychology* 7: 1–11.

INDEX

164

Printed in Great Britain
by Amazon